# A Guided Inquiry Approach to Teaching the Humanities Research Project

Randell K. Schmidt, Emilia N. Giordano, and Geoffrey M. Schmidt

Foreword by Carol C. Kuhlthau

Libraries Unlimited Guided Inquiry

 LIBRARIES
UNLIMITED™

An Imprint of ABC-CLIO, LLC
Santa Barbara, California • Denver, Colorado

**Library of Congress Cataloging-in-Publication Data**

Schmidt, Randell K.
  A guided inquiry approach to teaching the humanities research project / Randell K. Schmidt, Emilia N. Giordano, and Geoffrey M. Schmidt ; foreword by Carol C. Kuhlthau.
      pages cm. — (Libraries unlimited guided inquiry)
  Includes bibliographical references and index.
    ISBN 978-1-4408-3438-7 (pbk : acid-free paper) — ISBN 978-1-4408-3439-4 (ebook)
    1. Humanities—Research—Methodology.  2. Humanities—Study and teaching (Secondary)  3. Report writing—Study and teaching (Secondary)  4. Inquiry-based learning.  I. Giordano, Emilia N.  II. Schmidt, Geoffrey.  III. Title.
    AZ186.S388  2015
    001.3072'1—dc23        2015012909

ISBN: 978-1-4408-3438-7
EISBN: 978-1-4408-3439-4

19  18  17  16  15      1  2  3  4  5

This book is also available on the World Wide Web as an eBook.
Visit www.abc-clio.com for details.

Libraries Unlimited
An Imprint of ABC-CLIO, LLC

ABC-CLIO, LLC
130 Cremona Drive, P.O. Box 1911
Santa Barbara, California 93116-1911

This book is printed on acid-free paper ∞
Manufactured in the United States of America

*For Donna, Debbie, Betsy, Janice, Tina, and Marishka—friends and sisters all.*
*—RKS*

*To my parents, Sal and Bettina, who showed me at the earliest possible age that*
*The World is Our Classroom. And to my great-grandmother and grandmother,*
*Carmela and Annemarie, whose belief that I could do anything*
*I set my mind to sent me on this path.*

*—ENG*

*With respect for all the students and staff I have worked with*
*at Passages Academy, IDP, ROADs, and PCA.*

*—GMS*

# Contents

# Foreword

An important challenge for high school educators is to prepare their college-bound students for success in undergraduate work. Students making the transition to college frequently find academic research especially difficult to master. Even students that have experience with term papers, extended essays, and capstone projects in high school are often confused and overwhelmed when confronted with their first academic research paper. This book presents a workshop for guiding students in the steps of producing a research paper in the humanities, especially for students planning to engage in university study.

Over more than a decade Randell Schmidt and her colleagues at Gill St. Bernard School have developed a systematic program that has successfully and consistently led their students to research independence and academic success and had a powerful impact on the entire school. Randi and her coauthors share their expertise in this practical guide for teachers and librarians that is aligned with the seven stages of the Information Search Process and the Common Core State Standards.

This book is an addition to the Guided Inquiry series that is based in my research on students' process of learning from a variety of sources described in the Information Search Process (ISP) (*Seeking Meaning*, Kuhlthau, 2004). The foundational text in the series is *Guided Inquiry: Learning in the 21st Century*, 2nd edition (Kuhlthau, Maniotes, and Caspari, 2015).

This addition to the Guided Inquiry series is a companion to two other books by Schmidt and her colleagues, *Teaching the Scientific Literature Review: Collaborative Lessons for Guided Inquiry* (2014) and *A Guided Inquiry Approach to High School Research* (2013). Taken together these texts offer a workshop program for developing high school students into independent academic scholars. These books make a daunting task manageable through tested lessons that provide guidance at each stage in the ISP. The high school students that have gone through the program found that they were well prepared to make the transition to college research and report that this was a critical part of their high school education that prepared them for college work.

Carol C. Kuhlthau, Professor Emerita
Rutgers, the State University of New Jersey

# Preface

## *On Guided Inquiry-Based Learning and the Common Core in a Humanities Research Project*

In precollegiate education two very important concepts are rising in prominence: inquiry-based learning and the Common Core Standards. Each concept speaks to a dramatic shift in schools, the information environment, and indeed how children come to know themselves and the world in which they live.

The book you are now reading was written by three educators who embrace the idea that a high school student can learn better in today's information-rich environment if guided research can be accomplished after a personal inquiry is decided upon. And once the personal inquiry is established, using the curriculum outlined in this book, the grade-level standard in language arts and history can easily be matched to the expectations of the Common Core State Standards.

The origin of the research project that is modeled in the book is a scaffolded English language research paper. The guided inquiry-based unit is assigned over a nine- to twelve-week period in a tenth-grade American literature course. Teachers and librarians serve as research and writing guides throughout the guided inquiry. The paper's assignment, and especially its focus upon literary and artistic figures and their influence upon American culture, has evolved over the past fifteen years to include not only men and women in literature or fine arts but also historical, social, technological, and political figures, ideas, and movements. Thus, the assignment has extended from the world of literature and fine arts into many other aspects of the humanities including history, architecture, religion, and photography and has become a more inclusive research project in the humanities.

In fact, if we were to inspect the breadth of the sixteen interrogation sheets included within the book, most of the interrogations address materials not typically found in purely literary research and analysis, but often found in historical, geo-political, or social research and analysis. Therefore, the book and the assignment model can easily be applied to various social studies courses as well as English language courses. In addition, student handouts throughout the book can be used for stand-alone lessons in the humanities apart from a cohesive research project.

While twenty structured workshops are provided in the book, all but one lasting for a fifty-minute period, other unstructured workshops of fifty minutes' duration are suggested throughout the assigned unit. The unstructured workshop times are meant to be supervised in-class work time to conduct additional research, finish the work of the previous workshop, continue note-taking, prepare for the next phase of research, or consult with the teacher, librarian, or study buddy for extra help. All of the workshops, both structured and unstructured, are under the watchful eyes of the teacher and librarian guides.

The organization of this book is straightforward. The first six chapters constitute Part I: The Teacher's Practicum, which explains the nature of the assignment and the shift toward a modern guided inquiry approach to assigning, teaching, and assessing the humanities research project.

The second section of the book, Part II, contains twenty workshops in sequence. Each workshop has three parts. The first part is the overview for the teacher, which explains the workshop lesson and provides the teacher with background information to conduct the workshop. Part two is the workshop plan, which lays out steps, materials, and logistics of the students' structured work times. The third part of each workshop is the student handout(s) to be disseminated or adapted as the teacher and librarian determine.

Some handouts are helpful guides for students to use to find resources. Some handouts are step-by-step guides to accomplish the research task being taught in the workshop and some handouts are to be filled out by the student, to help the student work through a research task. All the handouts are particularly designed for student use and are meant to be helpful not as assessments or preparations for assessment but primarily to help the researcher *learn* how to research. Each handout is intended to be copied by the teacher or librarian and used by the student.

The last section of the book is the Appendices, which unites with the Teacher' Practicum to provide the teacher and librarian with the tools needed to train for, plan, teach, and assess the humanities research paper using a guided inquiry approach. In the Appendices are a plan for professional development for the project and the SLIM packet, which sets up a three-stage self-assessment for the student and project knowledge development assessment for the teacher. Sample project assessment sheets for teacher usage are also included.

## Special Note for History Teachers on Historical Thinking, Reading, and Writing

The project described in this book is intended for a humanities classroom employing requisite skills of literary, historical, and social analysis. However, this project can be adapted to fulfill a more defined disciplinary literacy approach by incorporating historical reading and writing skills. By choosing to identify, teach, and assess specific Historical Thinking Skills or Social Studies Practices the humanities research project is easily transformed into a more directed history research paper rather than a holistic humanities project. While the scope of the book is not specifically historical research, it is worth identifying resources to support historical and social studies disciplinary literacy in general, and historical thinking in particular, as they can apply to this project.

Tim Shanahan and Cynthia Shanahan of the University of Illinois at Chicago write that disciplinary literacy is a specific literacy practice separate from content area reading. Whereas content area reading applies general literacy strategies to learn discipline-based content, disciplinary literacy, "is an emphasis on the knowledge and abilities possessed by those who create, communicate and use knowledge within the discipline" (Shanahan and Shanahan, 2012, 8).

There is a variety of sources for information on historical thinking skills, including the Stanford History Education Group; University of Maryland, Baltimore County's Center for History Education: Assessment Resource Center for History; and University of California at Los Angeles: National Center for History in the Schools. Although each organization defines historical thinking in its own particular way dependent upon research and practice, all agree that the skills should not be practiced in isolation. The National Center for History in the Schools, which identifies and describes five historical thinking standards—Chronological Thinking, Historical Comprehension, Historical Analysis and Interpretation, Historical Research Capabilities, and

Historical Issues—Analysis and Decision-Making, explains that the standards, "while presented in five separate categories, are nonetheless **interactive and mutually supportive**" (National Center for History in the Schools at UCLA, 1996).

In addition to describing the standards, all three organizations identify ways to integrate historical thinking into instruction. Sam Wineburg, head of the Stanford History Education Group (SHEG) and author of *Historical Thinking and Other Unnatural Events* (2001), coauthored (with Daisy Martin and Chauncey Monte-Sano) *Reading Like a Historian* (2013). *Reading Like a Historian* presents eight chapters with lessons teaching particular historical thinking concepts. For example, a chapter with the Core Question* "Was Lincoln a racist?" teaches contextualization (Wineburg, Martin, and Monte-Sano, 2013, p. ix). To support assessing historical thinking, each group also provides examples of assessment as well assessment tools such as rubrics. Perhaps the strongest support is a rubric provided by UMBC: Center for History Education Assessment Resource Center for History (ARCH). ARCH offers an elementary and secondary rubric that integrates SHEG's research as well as the work of leading researcher Bruce VanSledright from *Assessing Historical Thinking and Understanding: Innovative Ideas for New Standards* (2014).

## Websites on Historical Thinking:

Historical Thinking Matters (a collaboration between Sam Wineburg and the late Roy Rosenzweig): http://historicalthinkingmatters.org/

National Center for History in the Schools at UCLA: http://www.nchs.ucla.edu/history-standards/historical-thinking-standards

Stanford History Education Group: http://sheg.stanford.edu/home_page

Teaching History.org (examples of historical thinking): http://teachinghistory.org/best-practices/examples-of-historical-thinking

UMBC: Center for History Education Assessment Resource Center for History (rubrics): http://www.umbc.edu/che/arch/rubric.php

*The authors welcome any questions or comments regarding this guided inquiry approach to teaching the humanities research project.*

**A final note on gender-neutral language: While the authors believe that gender-neutral language is entirely appropriate in the classroom, its use in a text is sometimes awkward and often confusing. Rather than adopting an even distribution of he/she pronouns throughout, the authors have adopted the traditional male pronoun usage for the purpose of applying that use with no gender partiality intended.**

---

* SHEG's terminology; also known as a focus question.

# Acknowledgments

Guided Inquiry as a method of teaching students how to access, assess, and assimilate information to build their own new knowledge is gaining traction in high schools in the United States and other countries. Because the method can be used with multidisciplinary content and taught at different ages and developmental stages, guided inquiry is poised to become a central feature of high school classes in which research is an expected or required activity.

This book, like the previous two books I have authored or coauthored, extends Kuhlthau's Information Search Process theory into teaching, in this case into the commonly assigned humanities research project. In keeping with the many disciplines of the humanities, the book was produced only through the efforts of a large cast of characters—teachers, students, curriculum designers, manuscript readers, editors—all of them people interested in furthering teaching and learning through the humanities research project.

Emilia, Geoffrey, and I wish to thank the folks whose expertise deepens student interaction with the information being researched and who have contributed interrogation sheets for a variety of sources. The interrogation sheets open an innovative avenue for the student to travel and learn more precisely from a given source and to obtain more meaningful information for his/her research project.

So thanks go to Interrogation Sheet creators: Derek Martin, Sarah Isusi, Jennifer Diamond, Andrew Lutz, Paul Canada, Cindy Orr, Goran Brolund, David Southerland, Laurence Bostian, Lee Fitzgerald, Robert Ort, John Ripton, William Diamond, Kristen Armstrong, and Margery Schiesswohl. With the exceptions of Goran and Lee who teach in Sweden and Australia, respectively, all the other creators are Gill St. Bernard's teachers.

Thanks also to Joseph Schmidt, senior instructional specialist for the New York City Department of Education, for his contributions on metacognition and historical resources. We thank students Isabelle Demontigny and Sandy Gooen for their comments and criticism during the book's development as well as the entire GSB senior class of 2015 for the tips they gave us. Manuscript readers Christina Selheimer, Cynthia Washburn, Stephanie Back, and Cecilia Rhodes are thanked for their patience, their expertise with the English language, and their eagle eyes for catching flaws in the manuscript.

I am especially appreciative of the Gill St. Bernard's English department members for their educational perspective and help in organizing the book, the initial assignment sheet which we have adapted, and grading rubrics which we have included as well as grappling with us about pedagogical issues. A shout-out of thanks goes to English teacher Sharon Poticny for early discussion of the organization of the book and the levels of assessment, and to English teachers Andrew Lutz and Derek Martin and history teacher Candace Pryor Brown for later discussions on pedagogy and how a paper is organized. My appreciation also goes to Amy Mai Tierney for her cooperation in helping to create our first interrogation sheets in the ninth-grade research book, especially as regards to interviews. As always, a great debt is owed to assistant librarian Claudia Hesler who created the database lesson and handout and a sample list of resources.

Claudia has made an art of steadfast resource support and so gracefully steers the library though the storms of teenage research angst.

To our editor, Sharon Coatney: it has been an absolute joy working with you over the years. I have learned so much about education, pedagogy, and publishing, and I have always appreciated your gentle ways.

We constantly remind our students that they stand on the shoulders of previous knowledge creators. I, too, stand on the shoulders of many, many humanitarians. But those who have most contributed to my understanding of how children learn are my husband, lifelong educator Peter Schmidt; my sons, public school educators Joseph and Geoffrey Schmidt; my coauthor and former student and media whiz, Emilia Giordano; and my mentor, Carol C. Kuhlthau. I am humbled by all that you all know and by what you have given me. My thanks to you!

*Randell K. Schmidt*

# Teacher's Practicum

# The Traditional Humanities Research Paper

A research project in the humanities has been a time-honored tradition in high school and early collegiate courses throughout the past fifty years. Such a project is taught to introduce students to scholarly research in history, language, arts, and social studies. A student completing a research project is expected to use multiple sources to explore existing information available about a certain topic, which is often assigned to him. Such exploration of multiple sources is expected to yield several pages in a research report of the topic. In addition to displaying some content of each of the sources, the paper also evokes and announces the student's own thesis or main idea that ties the materials together and provides evidence of how the thesis is manifest in those materials.

In other words, the humanities research paper introduces a student to how to look in old materials for an idea that he develops as a new thesis, and then how to write a report on the materials which should provide sufficient evidence for his thesis. Thus, the student discovers something new to think about by using multiple existing materials.

While the research project has evolved over the years to incorporate more types of sources and may have advanced past the stage of teacher-recommended subjects to allow for more independent, student-initiated inquiry, the expectations for the development of a thesis, as well as providing evidence to support the thesis, remain ingrained in high school research projects. However, with the expanding information landscape and the ubiquitous access to digitalized data, as well as increased scholarship on how students process information and how research is done more effectively, the old research protocols are giving way to new practices and methods for teaching the research process.

This book portrays an existing, newer method for teaching the research project. The authors will describe a comprehensive method for teaching the humanities research project to high school or early college students that is grounded in Kuhlthau's (1994) Information Search Process (ISP) and utilizing a Guided Inquiry approach to the project. This method incorporates student-generated interest in a subject with distinct lessons on information handling. The lessons inform the student of assignment expectations, particular source possibilities, strategies for using different types of sources, and methods of interacting with research materials through interrogation of textual and nontextual sources. Students then report on what was found in the research process in a paper, presentation, or creative project (Kuhlthau, Maniotes, and Caspari, 2007; Schmidt, 2013; Schmidt, Smyth, and Kowalski, 2014).

The research process utilized in this book is Kuhlthau's Information Search Process (**see figure 1.1**) which she describes as a seven-stage process of Initiation, Selection, Exploration, Formulation, Collection, Presentation, and Assessment. The Information Search Process, which was first portrayed in the 1980s and has consistently been cited as a scholarly, well-researched model for information-seeking behavior, was first identified by Kuhlthau in research she completed while studying New Jersey high school students fulfilling a humanities research project assignment (Kuhlthau, 2004).

Since that time, the Information Search Process study has been continuously replicated by other researchers with subjects of different ages, occupations, and research situations. The seven stages of information seeking and the three levels of informational behaviors that Kuhlthau first described have been evidenced in other replicated subject groups (Kuhlthau, 2004).

Thus, the workshops within this book will be divided into the seven stages of the ISP and labeled:

Research in the Initiation Stage of the Information Search Process
Research in the Selection Stage of the Information Search Process
Research in the Exploration Stage of the Information Search Process
Research in the Formulation Stage of the Information Search Process
Research in the Collection Stage of the Information Search Process
Research in the Presentation Stage of the Information Search Process
Research in the Assessment Stage of the Information Search Process

The book's Appendices will provide an outline for a professional development program on the Guided Inquiry approach to humanities research, as well as other supporting documents.

# The Rise of the Research Question and the Decline of the Thesis

In this chapter let us start with a simple question that involves a mysterious phrase. How can a high school or early college student, who is a neophyte researcher and who exhibits an "anomalous state of knowledge" (Belkin, 1980, 133), possibly formulate a thesis early in the research process?

The idea of creating a thesis and finding sources of support for that thesis, which then becomes the body of a research paper in the humanities, is a practice that is losing ground in the new environment of broad and digitalized information. In this world of exponential knowledge development and distribution, the contemporary student who does not even know what he does not know and is in an anomalous state of knowledge, cannot clearly formulate a thesis precise enough to enter a narrow subject into a search engine. With no precise thesis, how does the student receive an information set from the search engine tailored to specifically address his subject? The modern student, who might formulate an imprecise thesis, will find himself inundated with database entries and will be incapable of determining where to begin and how to handle those entries, particularly if the entries are scholarly in nature and deal with highly specific responses to his haphazard thesis. A thesis, after all, is predicated on enough prior knowledge and understanding of the subject matter to allow the student to formulate his own question about the subject, and with that question propose or theorize a response to the question that he can then support with researched evidence that he has found (Belkin, 1980, 133).

The old expectation of emphasizing a thesis in introductory humanities research in high school has never been easy to fulfill. Students would often rely upon humanities teachers to assist them both in formulating a thesis and looking for resources that would support or negate that thesis. While there is something commendable about a teacher-student dialogue in the development of the thesis, oftentimes the thesis developed would remain somewhat of an abstraction to the student researcher who would set out in the hunt for evidence to support a thesis that he might not have even developed himself and might not yet fully understand. This situation does not engender critical or deep thinking. Instead the paper becomes just another long and confusing assignment.

The position held by the authors of this book encourages a more organic approach to initiating the research. We do not require a thesis to be developed in the first half of the process. Instead we ask the student to formulate a very simple question or, basically, state a topic he is interested in studying, because we know that most new student researchers know little or nothing substantive about their chosen topic. We encourage student choice of subject matter and we ask that only a simple question about that subject or a statement of interest in a topic form the initial basis of the research query.

Teachers and librarians then guide the student from an anomalous state of knowledge to the formulation of a more complex research question. By the middle of the research process the teacher and librarian will guide the student to a more specific thesis statement based upon both already completed and continuing research.

# The Information Search Process, Guided Inquiry, and the Workshops

During the last quarter of the 20th century, as computers and digital information gathering, storage, and searching came to the fore, a former high school librarian began scholarship on how high school students in New Jersey actually conducted a research project. Her study examined how, on a step-by-step and task-by-task basis, a particular group of students conducted a humanities research project resulting in a paper. What her research showed was that students engage in such an assignment on three levels: the affective level of feelings experienced, the cognitive level of thoughts during the research, and the physical level of actions taken to accomplish the research. As a result of her findings, Kuhlthau describes seven different stages of the research process, which she calls the "Information Search Process" (ISP), and provides a model for the ISP. See figure 1.1 below for the ISP model (Kuhlthau, 2004, 82).

While the Information Search Process originally described how high school students conducted their research, Kuhlthau and other scholars have shown that the same model describes the feelings, thoughts, and actions of people conducting research in other walks of life, at different ages and educational levels (Kuhlthau, 2004).

Kuhlthau remains a frequently cited library and information science scholar and continues to publish her work. This book utilizes her ISP model to suggest a guided inquiry approach to initial humanities research at the high school and early collegiate levels. As Kuhlthau and other scholars of inquiry-based learning continue to examine and write about how people search for and interact with new information, and particularly how students most successfully conduct

| Model of the Information Search Process (ISP) | | | | | | |
|---|---|---|---|---|---|---|
| | Initiation | Selection | Exploration | Formulation | Collection | Presentation | Assessment |
| Feelings (Affective) | Uncertainty | Optimism | Confusion Frustration | Clarity | Sense of direction/ confidence | Satisfaction or disappointment | Sense of accomplishment |
| Thoughts (Cognitive) | Vague ——————————————→ Focused | | | | Increased interest | | Increased self-awareness |
| Actions (Physical) | Seeking relevant information | | | | Seeking pertinent information | | |
| | Exploring | | | | Documenting | | |

Kuhlthau (2004, p. 82)

research, a positive and cooperative approach has developed for teaching students about research skills and new information handling. Kuhlthau, Maniotes, and Caspari (2007) indicate that this Guided Inquiry approach does not set curriculum but enhances the teaching of curriculum by recognizing the central role the information search process has in learning, particularly learning through inquiry. As they describe it, Guided Inquiry allows students to learn and teachers to teach content while employing a process of information discovery and assimilation (Kuhlthau, Maniotes, and Caspari, 2007).

The Guided Inquiry approach to humanities research found in this book reflects the ISP and begins at the Initiation Stage of the ISP, with the student receiving the assignment, continuing through the topic selection, exploration of information on the topic, formulation of the borrowed information into a simple research question, and collection of information from sources that provide material for the body of the paper. The Guided Inquiry then proceeds to the presentation of the materials and information collected and ends at the assessment stage after turning in the work to a teacher, with both the teacher and the student then determining what was learned in the research.

A key feature of the Guided Inquiry approach are the roles of the student, the teacher, and the librarian. Each is a partner to the others. This is not the old-fashioned banking system of education. In that system the student (hopefully) opens his head and the teacher (definitely) pours all the information needed to research and write the paper into the student's head. Rather, in a Guided Inquiry, a student initiates a topic or a simple question to be researched. The teacher, who may never have researched the topic and who may know little about it, understands, however, the process of information searching. Collaborating with the librarian, the teacher is able to guide the student through the ISP to the types of sources to investigate and teach the student how to mine the information from the sources. The teacher then assists the student in organizing the mined information to reflect upon and present in a research product.

It is the student claiming ownership of the inquiry, however, who benefits from the guidance. Perhaps the single most important factor in the modern-day humanities research project is the inquiry or question—however vaguely or roughly initially formed—that a student brings to the project. With so much information accessible and so little background information known by most students prior to the assignment, the student who expresses a personal interest in the topic and who is willing to pursue the inquiry because he is interested and curious is more likely to partner with his teacher and librarian to be guided through a successful project.

Thus, the student, although he is new to the research subject and to the research process initially, in a rudimentary fashion and later in an articulated statement, indicates his topic and begins to form the question(s) he wants to answer. As the Guided Inquiry unfolds for each student, the inarticulated research subject becomes an articulated research question, and the student researcher experiences an empowering ability to use borrowed information to help understand and learn about a topic, eventually formulating some of his own original ideas and creating a thesis about the inquiry he is pursuing.

While the Guided Inquiry approach is quite labor intensive for the teacher and collaborating librarian in the first stages of the information search process, so, too, it is intensive for the neophyte researcher. Research is hard work. As the student becomes acquainted with the unknown wilderness of information, sources such as those published in online databases demand patient searching strategies. Nontextual sources are also myriad and often confusing. Students who may be quite media savvy (even more so than their teachers) are nonetheless new to accessing, assessing, and assimilating various information formats in multiple media for scholarly purposes. For these reasons, the humanities project is a partnership between student, teacher, and librarian.

Teachers, take heart because as the research proceeds and the students who are invested in their own choices of subject begin to experience the surprise, joy, and satisfaction of their efforts, the research process burden shifts to the shoulders of the student researcher. For example, he may meet with the teacher to say he is changing the focus of his research, or he will ask the librarian for more sources, or he will complain that he has too many notecards and too much information! With each discussion the teacher or librarian guides the student to another source, the next step, or a different articulation of his research. More and more the labor intensifies for the student researcher. Teachers and librarians then experience the birth of a new scholar.

# Interrogation of Sources and the Development of a Researcher's Ideas by Directly Questioning the Materials

Research—that is, searching for, assimilating, and reporting information—is an activity that is easier for some students to learn than it is for others. In our experience, humanities teachers as a group tend to fall into the category of those who, when they were students, enjoyed research and did not think it difficult or mysterious. While not trying to stereotype all history, English, or social studies teachers—because certainly some did not understand or enjoy research—we are making a point. If a teacher has found research to be an easy and even enjoyable undertaking as a student and later as an adult, and if that teacher has developed his or her own natural system of undertaking and organizing that research, then such a teacher may assume that most students will naturally undertake research and find their own comfort level in handling large amounts of previously unvisited materials and information. With this perspective, the humanities teacher will often lead the class to the library, listen as the librarian explains database searching, and then set the students free to do their own thing. The teacher will assume that true, in-depth research will take place and that each student will find useful material and borrow information from it that might spur his own new ideas. The teacher may assume that notes will be made from the borrowed information and that the student will dig deeply into the materials to make sure that the research is more than superficial. The teacher will think that enough information has been borrowed and thought about to produce a critical analysis of the texts or other sources involved and of the ideas portrayed in those sources.

Those optimistic humanities teachers, in a brief and cautionary lesson, will explain the negative consequence of plagiarism and the positive results of citations but do little to model such scholarly behavior for their students and seldom discuss the Western tradition of scholarly protocols and the advancement of human knowledge through research.

Recently a veteran history teacher was asked how her current students did on their research assignment. Her reply was startling: "I recently assigned a humanities research paper where the end results were superficial and ahistorical. Students clearly did not understand how to find sources and use sources that provided information for their analysis and answered their research question." The teacher's statement portrays a displeasure with the shallow materials used and the lack of in-depth research done. The teacher's response indicates a lack of information guidance, a failure of the humanities teacher and the librarian to teach fundamental skills of seeking, choosing, interrogating, and analyzing textual, visual, audio, and other materials integrally involved with the research question.

In fact, the teacher's response serves as a clarion call announcing the seismic shift in the information-seeking environment now occurring at the precollegiate and early college levels. At this time, so much information is available to access easily that the lead question shifts from, "How and where can I get my information for the project?" to "What do I do and how do I handle all of the information I might find? How do I assume meaning from it and how do I connect it to my research question?"

The time for solid collaborations between humanities teachers and information specialists in the library is at hand. Central to those collaborations is the agreement between teacher and librarian that students must learn what to do with all of the information they have available and how to interrogate that information to gain context and meaning.

Having taught research skills to high school students for two decades and having utilized a Guided Inquiry approach to teaching research for fifteen years, the authors know that a student can be guided through the stages of research described by Kuhlthau in her ISP model. But the student will be uncertain how to fully utilize the sources he has found, especially if those sources are not traditional textual sources or typical high school humanities sources.

By the second year of high school, most students are able to make notes from traditional lectures and texts, having learned these skills and practiced them in class. But frequently, such note-taking is done in the context of a body of knowledge and information in which the teacher and student are currently engaged. Thus, an American history student learns to take notes from historical texts used in class.

However, the student undertaking a new research project will probably have very little background knowledge of the information encountered in the obtained sources, many of which may be nontextual. The sources themselves, whether they are interviews, performances, textiles, or something else, may be unusual if not foreign to the student's experience and understanding of what is contained therein. For example, is there different information inherent in a fabricated uniform for the Civil War than there is in a photograph of that same uniform? Can a student learn something from viewing a work of art by Chuck Close that cannot be learned from a textual description of the same artwork? Is a vinyl recording of the opera *Madama Butterfly* going to provide the same experience in information handling as a live opera performance? And how does a neophyte researcher utilize and interact with several different vessels, or sources, of information to produce a cohesive and interesting research paper?

When a student interrogates a source, whether that source is text, graphic, human, textile, photograph, performance, music, artifact, or art, he asks direct questions to draw meaning from the material that a single read-through or first encounter may not produce. Those questions can be more fully answered by the student, and by asking the questions he is taking the time to more deeply examine the material, material which quite often is foreign to his knowledge base and may demand a more concentrated effort than a simple reading or cursory interaction.

In his interrogation through direct questions, the student researcher confronts answers directly from the material and may then use these answers as research materials, making notes on them and eventually choosing to use or discard the notes in preparing to present the research in a paper or other format. When his notes are made of the questions and answers from, for example, a photograph, the photograph is just as legitimate a source as textual sources, and the notes are real research notes. The information the researcher receives in the interrogation can be cross-referenced or compared to other information from other sources in other formats. The student researcher may, indeed, have to look at other sources in other formats to answer more thoroughly some of the questions he is using to interrogate the photograph itself, especially if the student is totally unfamiliar with the photograph or the photographer. A good example might be the portrait photographer, Richard Avedon. Many of his portrait photographs share light backgrounds and a similar subject's stance. The student might want to know something of Avedon's style prior to interrogating an Avedon photograph.

Teachers and librarians should understand that no single set of questions suggested as interrogations will necessarily satisfy the research assignment. They are intended as prompts or as guiding questions which, as the student interacts with them, will enable the student to formulate further questions. Thus, the student comes to "own" the interrogation and gain confidence in his ability to formulate questions from the sources.

As different sources are interrogated with questions, the researcher receives more information to think about regarding the research topic. Because the researcher is actively interacting with sources he may simultaneously be creating some of his own original ideas from the suggested questions or from his own original questions. The student researcher is then better able to narrow or broaden the focus of the research topic and more deeply identify or define the question or questions that are driving his research.

The concept of interacting with an information source shifts the student researcher's behavior from a passive recipient of information to an active investigator of information. If a student can be shown or taught how to interrogate (question) various information sources then the student's interactions with the sources become livelier. By interrogating a source, a student researcher asks specific questions of the source he is handling and then based on his own observations and his own experiences with that source, he answers the question he has asked. For example, if a student finds a blog post he may ask questions about why that blog post was written or whether the content was logical.

If a teacher or librarian can guide the student to ask some initial basic questions, even though these questions are suggested by the teacher because the student is unable to formulate the questions by himself, the student's answers to those questions may arouse the student's curiosity and instigate other questions that originate in the student's own mind. These other questions may be addressed to the original source being questioned or may require the student to seek other sources for answers. Herein is the essence of scholarship.

To further understand the need to interrogate sources so that students can better interact with the research materials, let us examine some nontextual high school research sources. As a more nuanced understanding about learning styles, which are first described in Howard Gardner's 2011 work *Frames of Mind: The Theory of Multiple Intelligences* and later revisited in his 1999 *The Disciplined Mind* (76–79), takes hold, many educators are embracing the concept of using nontextual sources to enhance the research experience for their students. For the student who is a kinesthetic learner, physical activities, performances, and three-dimensional objects are possible study subjects in the digital environment as well as in the physical world. A teacher or librarian guide will recognize the importance of the interplay between the learner and the kinesthetic information sources. So, the student who is interested in studying the history of modern-day soccer competition may now view the historic upset of Brazil's national team by Germany's national team in the quarter finals of the FIFA 2014 World Cup games in Brazil. The student may examine Youtube clips, listen to an interview with a coach from Brazil, study stop-action photographs of key plays, or watch the entire game re-broadcast on a major network in Spanish or English. *Realia*, which are physical objects (such as those found in museums and exhibitions) directly related to the subject, can and should also be considered for interrogation. All of these sources can be interrogated with a few simple, basic questions that the student will then answer, the answer becoming the textual notes to be incorporated into his final report of research.

For the artistic student who may also be an auditory learner and wants to know the relationship between the use of heavy makeup and the success of the rock band KISS, nontextual sources may provide a deeper and more satisfying research experience. In the current era, high school and college students are very familiar with nontextual sources and often use nontextual sources for information seeking, whether through social media such as Facebook or Pinterest, interactive events such as live streams or flash mobs, or media delivered through image, radio, or video. Students can also interact with nontextual sources such as realia found in a visit to a vintage shop, a museum, or a field experience.

With this deepening interaction between student and source, the research project often experiences a shift in ownership. The student takes charge of the information search as the knowledge the student encounters grows and his own newer ideas about the research topic take shape.

Three workshops (**Workshops 4, 7, and 13**) contain the prototypes for interrogating different, particularly nontextual, sources. These prototypes are found on interrogation sheets for each of the following nontextual sources:

Interrogation of Social Media Content
Interrogating a Work of Art
Interrogating a Coin or Pottery Sherd
Interrogating a Garment
Interrogating a Graph
Interrogating in an Interview
Interrogating a Live or Recorded Musical Performance
Interrogating a Natural Phenomenon
Interrogating a Photograph
Interrogating a Political Cartoon
Interrogating a Live or Recorded Speech, or a Transcript of a Speech
Interrogating a Live or Recorded Sporting Event
Interrogating a Live or Recorded Theater Performance

Textual document interrogation sheets will include the following:

Interrogating an Allusion
Interrogating a Nonfiction Text Which Is an Encyclopedia (General or Specialized)
Interrogating Realistic Fiction
Interrogating a Legal Document
Interrogating a Textual Source of Nonfiction

Each interrogation sheet within this book was created by a content teacher who uses the information source being interrogated in regular high school classes. For example, a Latin teacher who is trained in archeology created the interrogation sheet for a coin or pottery sherd while a photography teacher created the interrogation sheet for the photograph. In all, **sixteen** interrogation sheets are enclosed. Others may be created by the humanities teacher and added as students identify those sources they choose to incorporate into their projects. Most importantly, nontextual sources have become more accessible and useful as the student hones his interrogation skills and practices concentrated interactions with his sources, thus enhancing the opportunity to generate new insights and original thoughts on his research topic.

# Media Literacy and the Role of Social Media

*If human beings form a social network it is not because they interact with other human beings. It is because they interact with human beings and endless other materials too.*

John Law (382)

## Media Literacy

It is predicted that in 2015, students will be exposed to 15.5 hours of media each day (Short, 2013). Information overload begins with the barrage of information that students are automatically expected to deflect and filter on a daily basis. This information arrives to the student through texts, photographs, videos, and audio and is disseminated through traditional mass media (television and radio broadcasts, print and digital publications) and social media, via a variety of vehicles such as mobile devices and personal computers.

The rise of social media and lifestyle branding has dissolved the boundary between voluntary and involuntary media consumption. Social sharing platforms and the affordability of communication devices have created an environment of constant connectivity. Hyperlinks that connect the user to content on a different page of the same website or to another page of a different website constitute hypermediation (Bolter and Grusin, 2000, 30). Hypermediation has fostered a culture of nonstop information overload. One search for a simple topic can result in a class period of unproductive tangential browsing. While the process of unstructured browsing is a highly important step of the Information Search Process, especially in the beginning when the student begins to develop an inarticulated question, a haphazard approach can easily waste time.

As media evolves and occupies our attention, almost every media outlet has a social sharing strategy for marketing and branding. Shaped by pop-culture adolescent branding, students may not realize that the network of their social contacts and interactions with information is insular; that is, a network that does not provide a diverse information set. While feeds of information have evolved from fragmented bits to highly curated campaigns designed to hold the attention of adolescents over time, social media draws students into subconscious brand identification.

A lack of information and media literacies is typically shown in the student's rush to connect with like-minded peers and products. Students ultimately engage in insular networks. Such networks commonly fulfill a commercial demand, a demand that students do not necessarily realize they are feeding. It is a demand that will not satisfy scholarly research needs. Insular networks feed narrow perspectives and biases that are conscious and unconscious, thus shifting the focus of the student from diverse sources of information to a cacophony of repetition from a narrower perspective.

Paradoxically, students are losing the ability to sustain focus and tend to shift from one device to the next and one platform to another, while simultaneously consuming a variety of other media. Jenkins in his report titled "Confronting the Challenges of Participatory Culture: Media Education for the 21st Century" makes a case for positive outcomes of "multitasking" (2006, 61). However, among young students, multitasking behaviors sometimes detract from the student's research process by pulling the focus away from the task at hand. For example, a student might be tasked with conducting research in the reference room but will divide his attention between music on an audio device, peeks at his social media profiles, and snapping photos to send to classmates in the classroom next door, while supposedly conducting his research. Student information-seeking behaviors typically involve passive absorption of publicized materials, rather than informed deconstruction of complex information structures. Much of the information that students locate or consume in superficial searches is irrelevant commercial content and does not serve the purpose of scholarship.

As students are taught media literacy regarding social media and learn how to seriously consider the information they find and choose meaningful data, they mature in their interactions with media and usage. But such maturity does not come at a predictable rate. Teaching media literacy skills is about a gradual acquisition from freshman year through senior year of media-handling skills. This problem does not just affect high school students. College students and even professionals experience the pitfalls of "media multitasking" and must discipline themselves to attend to the research task at hand.

The rapid circulation of commercial content has had unintended consequences in shaping student perceptions of information seeking. Content associated with lifestyle brands, sports, and entertainment (pop culture) is so readily available that students have a difficult time satisfying a challenging academic search in the classroom. For example, a student might assume that locating a primary source about an American Civil Rights march is as simple as locating the score of the previous night's Yankees game.

The notion that students of the information age are "digital natives" does not guarantee that they are media literate or naturally equipped with information seeking skills (Prensky, 2001, 1). For example, a student may have fulfilled the task of establishing a topic of his choice but may not know how to launch a sophisticated search. The student interested in researching the destruction of the Amazon Rainforest may only enter the keywords "Chevron" and "Amazon" into a vague Google search. Launching a search with ambiguous keywords may generate unintended results, such as the Chevron Company's website or books for sale at Amazon.com. To address this common mistake, a librarian would have to explain the use of natural language in mainstream search engines and the application of search algorithms and techniques that will potentially maximize or minimize the value of the students' search terms. This common mistake could take an entire class period to address if students are not cumulatively building media and information literacies. This book begins to address essential media education topics in its exposition of the student's research process.

Until students are taught foundational information, media, and technology literacies, they will be subject to an endless merry-go-round, or closed feedback loop. Thus, it is the role of the librarian to help students penetrate through insular networks and open the door to new networks of multiple information sources while shifting student perspectives to encompass all types of information sources, both textual and nontextual, digital, and print. Once this perspective is gained, students can then begin to analyze and decode the messages contained in their acquired information sources. Herein lies the ability to think critically in today's hyper-connected information environment.

The student learns to ask questions such as:

What language was used in the source?
Do the lighting techniques in a film clip reflect the mood of a scene?
Do the design choices of a presidential bumper sticker reflect the candidate's position?
How does the style of editing in a documentary reveal the documentarian's perspective?
Does a wardrobe change during a play indicate class?
Can you detect editorial control of a newspaper article?
What television network broadcasted the program you are examining? Who has access to that
    program? Who does not have access to that program?

The ability to intentionally divide one's attention among many formats and delivery methods of information, and simultaneously focus on the method, the message, and the ramifications of that delivery and message, encompasses the essence of media literacy.

## The Library as the Hub

Librarians and their carefully curated libraries can be viewed as the hub of an information network and the transfer point for existing and new knowledge. Information networks consist of relational and evolving conditions that permit and/or inhibit information flow through social and nonsocial interactions. Within a network are "actors" who customize the provisions and access to information. In the library network, the "actors" are the librarians and support staff, individual teachers and teaching teams, study buddies, and individual students. The actors are equally as important as the *information sources*, which are print, digital, multimedia, textual, nontextual, and cultural artifacts that convey and hold information (Law, 1992, 398).

In the library, the interactive environment created between the "actors" and durable material—in human, cultural, conceptual, mechanical, and digital manifestations—can be called a *network*. *Durable materials* are significant products of an author's, or creator's, interaction with social connections, tools, and unlimited channels of information (Law, 1992, 381). Publications such as books, scholarly articles, and reference items are considered durable materials. Paintings, musical works, and sculptures are durable materials. Informational resources such as maps, textbooks, and manuals are durable materials. Each library has its own unique set of durable materials, curated with the taste and expertise of the librarian. Therefore, a larger network including and extending outside the library can be described to students as that which contains the natural and cultural world.

This world is made up of multitudinous, many-layered relational information networks. To teach a student how to research on different levels within multiple networks is to teach scholarly research skills that allow the student interactions with existing knowledge and the ultimate arrival at a higher, newer, more original understanding of that which he is researching.

A student with a developed understanding of these relational, interconnected networks can become an influential actor himself, able to create his own durable materials to add to an existing network or even to establish a new network. Thus the interaction between humans becomes equally important as the interaction with everything else, seen and unseen, in the network of life.

# Metacognition, Assessment, and Latitude: Measuring Growth

*Metacognition*, or the process of thinking about thinking, is one of the most difficult, and yet most important habits of mind to instill in adolescent learners. Almost by design, teenagers are wired to skip this step in the research process. The late Michael Martinez of the University of California Irvine School of Education stated that among all learners "cognition is sometimes, even often, carried out without much conscious deliberation" (2006, 697). Given the extemporaneous, even existential nature of teenagers, "conscious deliberation" by the teenager can be difficult. Therefore, it is important to develop the skills of metacognition just as you would develop other skills. The emphasis on process which is at the heart of a guided inquiry-based research project allows for the development of this often overlooked college-ready skill.

This book seeks to reinforce what Maribeth Schmitt and Timothy Newby of Purdue University define as the two components of metacognition; knowledge and regulation. In other words, metacognition involves an ability to understand personal strengths and weakness vis-à-vis the task and an ability to plan, monitor, and revise while acknowledging those strengths and weaknesses (Schmitt and Newby, 1986, 29–30). At several points in the humanities research project students are asked to plan, interrogate, and revise their research work. They are also expected to think about what and why they are learning during reflection time built into the workshops. Citing several studies on metacognition, Guy Trainin and H. Lee Swanson, when writing about students with learning disabilities, posit about all learners that "metacognition is not a set of idiosyncratic behaviors but a finite set of common skills that are highly correlated to academic success" (2005, 262). This humanities research project effectively highlights and builds on those skills in meaningful ways; when students are asked to think about successes and failures during the process, they are engaged in reinforcing metacognitive activities.

While it is understood that students who may not have much experience (or desire) in thinking about their own thinking may initially push back when asked to do so, it is important for them to be introduced to this larger skill. David Conley, a seminal theorist on college readiness, writes of the significance of metacognitive skills, including "self-management." Describing this skill he writes of the importance of the "development and use of new tools and techniques designed specifically to help us develop insight into student learning strategies. Gaining this type of insight would enable educators to teach students *how* to learn, as well as *what* to learn. It would also enable students to take more ownership and control over their own learning" (Conley, 2013, 21). The authors' hope is that this book offers a tool to teach students an important content skill of what to learn, as well as the research and metacognitive skills of *how* to learn.

Few educational endeavors are more difficult to quantify on a mass scale than growth in research skills and its manifestation in presentation skills, whether that presentation is an oral report, a paper, or a visual or three-dimensional creation. The assessment of how well students locate (access), determine the value of (assess), and utilize (assimilate) information, thus creating a meaningful research product, is difficult, especially when the product displays the individual's own Information Search Process, as well as each student's highly individualized creation of new knowledge through that process.

Teaching humanities research, writing, and presentation skills to high school and early college students is similar to teaching skills like cooking or swimming—skills that will be used throughout life on a regular basis and skills that will continue to enhance life as they are practiced and continue to improve as research deepens. Therefore, to assign a numerical grade to an individually measured but essential life skill is difficult.

Early in the 21st century, scholars at Rutgers University were grappling with the task as well. They began studies of the effects of trained librarians and guided inquiry curricula on student learning in New Jersey. For one of their studies, The School Library Impact Measure (SLIM) packet was produced with an instrument used to measure growth in the knowledge of the student moving through the Information Search Process, while doing research on a subject chosen in an established high school course (Todd, Kuhlthau, and Heinstrom, 2012, 1).

For our purposes, as we developed our own high school research and writing curriculum, we adopted the SLIM packet (see Appendix B, parts 1, 2, and 3) to chart content knowledge development and to begin the discussion of metacognition with our students. As the Rutgers scholars suggested, we administered the instrument to the students three times over the course of twelve weeks in a humanities research and writing course. In this course, approximately half of the lessons and the majority of assignments involved the completion of a research project of the student's own choosing and a six-minute presentation of the student's research findings. The SLIM instrument allowed the teacher and the student a snapshot of intellectual growth (that is, the development of a knowledge base about the subject and a processing of that knowledge to assimilate the information into a meaningful product) at three different stages of the process. We have continued to use the SLIM packet, recognizing it as a helpful assessment for both teacher and student (Todd, Kuhlthau, and Heinstrom, 2012, 1).

During this course other assessments were made of the student's work and we include a table for grading the actual presentation and a checklist of the project evaluation (see Appendix C). But the most telling assessments were the student responses in episodically administered SLIM instruments—the first filled out in class just after the student chooses a topic, the second filled out mid-way through the note-taking, and the third filled out right after the presentations were completed. Comparing the individual student's answers between first, second, and third instrument provides a narrative in the student's own words of intellectual growth in the research process. And, as the Rutgers scholars explained, the very nature of the changes in student responses from first to third instrument provide the measure of intellectual growth and knowledge development. As students moved from one word or phrase, with simple and sometimes vague responses, to sentences and later full paragraph explanations complete with definitions, details, and even, in some cases, analysis of the information on the SLIM instrument, intellectual growth is evident (Todd, Kuhlthau, and Heinstrom, 2012, 1).

In our experience, a comparative study of the three instruments is the best singular measurement of knowledge development, especially because students fill out the instruments without the aid of any of their research materials, sources, or notes. The instruments individually also serve as in situ measurements, that is, a measurement of knowledge at the time of completion of the instrument. Therefore, quantifiable information is recorded (such as the student's description of what he knows at that moment about the subject), as are the student's own feelings about the research at the moment the instrument is filled out. At a glance, teacher and librarian can determine who is in deep trouble, who is on track, who is forging ahead, and who needs an intervention.

While the instruments are not graded per se, credit can be given for the effort of filling out the instrument and for the student's knowledge development from one instrument to the other. In this way, the student is being graded against his previous responses, not in relation to other students' work. We, however, chose to only give credit for effort in filling out the instrument.

Content teachers constantly grapple with fair assessment. In conversations with humanities educators regarding a research project, the consensus is that latitude in assessment is necessary because the students come to this project with an array of skills and learning styles that they display in the classroom. For many students, this assignment may be their first real extensive scholarly research project and students vary dramatically at the starting point of their research process. Because students are coming to the project with a variety of past information-handling experiences (or lack thereof), the teacher cannot assume an initial level playing field. The research project becomes one of the first opportunities to make a uniform playing field upon which the students learn necessary life skills. Students themselves also come with different expectations of the purpose of this unique project. Latitude in assessment helps to equalize experience, resulting in the development of a life skill for every student.

However, the issue of latitude also demands some measure of fairness in order to give grades for performance. Instruments, checklists, or rubrics can be applied. Whatever allows each student to demonstrate in some objective measure—for example, in sources used and notes taken—and whatever assessment permits the student to actively engage in the Information Search Process is acceptable. The student then understands that research is a process to be learned, which is, after all, the main goal of the assignment.

# Student Workshops

## Prelude to a Research Project

*Research opens up doors. Once I chose a topic that I liked, the research that came with the project gave me ideas for other papers. I became so interested in the research part of the paper that when it came time for me to actually write, I had so much to say. I think that a common misconception when beginning to write a paper is that the task is going to be long and tedious. In reality, discovering more about something I was interested in was fun and informative.*

Isabelle Demontigny
Gill St. Bernard's School, Class of 2015

The following is an example of the development of a simple research topic into a simple research question for a humanities project and how that simple question changes, and becomes better articulated as the student handles and processes information about the topic. *At each of the stages of the Information Search Process changes occur in the topic* from Initiation Stage through to Presentation Stage (Kuhlthau, 2004).

This example illustrates those changes:

Sandy, the student, is interested in philosophy and women. She is informed that she must write a research paper in her tenth-grade English course and that she may choose the topic. The only caveat is that the topic must reflect some influence on American culture.

The Information Search Process has seven stages:

1. At the first stage of the process (the **Initiation Stage**), Sandy is informed of the required paper and receives the assignment. At this stage, she begins thinking about a possible topic, but she has not yet chosen one. However, she is thinking about doing something about women, or maybe philosophy. She keeps thinking. She goes to the library and begins informally searching. She is uncertain of what she is searching for, so she may talk to her teacher or the librarian and ask about women and/or philosophy. Suggestions of possible topics might come from those discussions or from finding resources as she browses the library.

2. She finds a book that looks interesting, or a video or a poster—something that shows information about Hannah Arendt, who was a female philosopher. Sandy looks in

a database and finds some material on Hannah Arendt, which also looks good. She decides in the second stage of the Information Search Process (the **Selection Stage**) to research the philosophical work of Hannah Arendt. Except for the little information she has already found, she does not yet know enough to fashion a research question. Instead, she starts looking at a biographical encyclopedia, a book, or an article written by Arendt, and finally, some cultural criticism of Arendt's work. She might even search the social media for blogs on philosophy and Arendt.

3. In the third stage of the Information Search Process (the **Exploration Stage**), Sandy looks at sources in the humanities. She begins to fashion a simple question, for example: How did Hannah Arendt understand and describe the causes of the Holocaust? Now she begins to seriously handle her materials. She has begun taking notes from sources she has gathered.

4. As she begins note-taking, Sandy will also actively interrogate her information sources to dig deeper into the material and make notes that are substantial. She is now in the **Formulation Stage**. With these interrogations and note-taking, her body of knowledge grows and her perspective of Hannah Arendt may change to include how Arendt personally escaped the Nazi Holocaust and what her exile meant in her philosophical writing. She may learn that Arendt was a student and protégé of philosopher Martin Heidegger, who was considered by some to be anti-Semitic, and how Arendt reported on the Nuremberg trials for a United States publication when Nazi leaders were being prosecuted for crimes against humanity.

Now, a more detailed picture is emerging for Sandy about the philosopher Hannah Arendt and her work. She is therefore able to articulate a more complex question about her subject, the work of Hannah Arendt. That question now becomes, "What were the key experiences that Hannah Arendt had that contributed to her philosophical statements about the banality of evil in the Holocaust?"

5. Having formulated her search and articulated her research question, Sandy must collect (the **Collection Stage**) more information to provide deeper evidence that Hannah Arendt had experiences that helped her to understand and write about how evil can appear banal. As Sandy collects the information and fills in the holes she has identified in her research, she gathers three or more detailed bodies of evidence from her sources to help answer her research question. Choosing from her notes on each of these three (because the assignment calls for three) bodies of evidence, Sandy is now able to articulate a thesis using the evidence to answer her question. She will discard notes she does not use.

6. In the **Presentation Stage**, Sandy titles her paper and develops her thesis statement as she writes several paragraphs containing each of the three bodies of evidence: In this case, the philosophical effects of Arendt's personal escape; Arendt's writings as a result of her relationship with the philosopher Heidegger; and Arendt's reporting of the Nuremberg Trials. These paragraphs will support Sandy's thesis about Arendt's views on the banality of evil. Sandy will write her conclusion and then formalize her introduction which will include a "hook" to gain her reader's attention. Sandy's hook will be a quotation or statement from one of her sources that catches the attention of her

reader and draws the reader into her subject matter. She will then check her works cited page and citations. The paper is ready to be evaluated.

7. In the **Assessment Stage**, surely Sandy will receive high evaluations for a job well done and will feel satisfied with her research project. Sandy will reflect about what she has learned and how she accomplished her research.

# Research in the Initiation Stage of the Information Search Process

Workshop 1: What Are the Humanities and Why Study Them?
Workshop 2: The Assignment
Workshop 3: Encouraging a Variety of Sources and Formats
Workshop 4: Hunting for Information and Browsing for Ideas

The teaching team for the twenty structured workshops often consists, if possible, of three educational guides. In most workshops the three guides are the classroom (content) teacher, the librarian who acts as the information search expert, and a third guide who may be a classroom or library aide and assists students in need of more individual attention. In some cases, the third guide may be a content expert or older student who has previously been through the assignment. While three guides are optimal, especially as students initiate the process and find sources, many schools do not have the expansive resources for three guides in each class. Therefore, our recommendations call for flexibility.

The Initiation Stage contains four workshops that will introduce students to scholarship in the humanities, how to view and discuss the assignment, and finally, how to begin to think about how and where to find sources. During this stage uncertainty prevails, and the adult guides should provide positive feedback and friendly help.

# Workshop 1

## Overview: What Are the Humanities and Why Study Them?

As a concept, the term "humanities" has encompassed courses in English language arts and United States and World history as well as other social studies courses in the high school curriculum. Practically, the humanities is a field that focuses on the human condition and how it has been expressed in literature and through culture. This fact alone should make the field significant enough for all emerging citizens of a democracy to learn, research, and strive to understand deeply. Understanding the humanities can mean reaching back across centuries or even into the very recent past, to unfold human development and cultural trends, in order to make sense of our current conditions. Doing this means looking at society through a variety of perspectives and disciplines as well as through multiple modes of information and interrogation. That is what this guided inquiry project is about.

High schools across the United States utilize research in the humanities in English language arts; history, and social studies classes; as well as in a myriad of electives and Advanced Placement classes that require students to delve into issues of cultural significance. Students exposed to primary, secondary, and tertiary sources that are both multitextual and rich in content to explore, interrogate, and analyze, ideally begin to do the serious work of scholarship that sets the groundwork for college- and graduate-level research.

This project asks students to conduct deep interrogation for meaning and connection within multiple sources and to synthesize the knowledge they find. Many of these sources should be nonwritten forms of information and communication. The humanities, with messages of past events and past creations, are communicated not only through written media but also through song, dance, food, performance, sport, speech, image, and more. Vintage footage and photographic images of civil rights protestors being sprayed to the ground by fire hoses can be and often are as haunting for students when researching the civil rights era, as is Martin Luther King's well known *Letter From a Birmingham Jail. Fires in the Mirror*, Anna Deavere Smith's one-person play about the aftermath of the Crown Heights disturbances of 1991, may serve as a strong supplement for the *New York Times* articles from that era.

The deciphering of meaning behind what constitutes being human, and where the human condition currently drives us as a society, requires the thinking, questioning, deep analyses, and creation of new meaning that all high schools should demand of their students. It prepares future thinkers, future engineers of the economy, future teachers, artists, and competent citizens with the ability to interrogate what makes us human, as well as what drives cultures and societies. Researching the humanities through the Guided Inquiry approach allows students to question an aspect of the past or current events that are significant to their own interests or social concerns, and subsequently delve through multiple sources with a variety of meanings, to make sense of their world. This also develops new knowledge that may illuminate for each student a new understanding of what it means to be human.

The teacher may wish to share this overview with his students, as a handout.

## Workshop 1: What Are the Humanities and Why Study Them?

**Learning Goals:** The goal of this workshop is to introduce the students to the concept of the humanities as a field of study and to explain why it is important to study the humanities.
**Location:** Library
**Team:** Teacher, librarian, and resource guide
**Inquiry Unit:** Initiation and introduction to the research project, its sources, and impact
**Total Time:** 50 minutes

| | |
|---|---|
| **Starter**<br>Time: 15 minutes<br><br>Inquiry<br>Community | The teacher should start by passing out the text of Martin Luther King's "I Have a Dream" speech, which the students can read silently or aloud. The teacher can then discuss the concept of the humanities and why it is important to learn from scholarship in the humanities. If available, the video of Martin Luther King's speech should be shown and the teacher could read from an analysis or critique of the speech. Questions from the students as well as comments about the speech can be taken. |
| **Work Time**<br>Time: 20 minutes<br><br>Study Buddies | Students split up into pairs or groups of four and choose one of the possible humanities-related samples the teacher offers. This may be a painting, a book, a play, a textual explanation of an idea, a musical piece, a small artifact such as a garment or a sculpture, a piece of jewelry, an item of ethnic food, etc. The student groups will choose one sample and do a little bit of research in the library about the place of the item in contemporary culture and what it might mean for the students. The teacher, referring back to Martin Luther King's "I Have a Dream" speech, might refer to the racial inequality manifest in the response to the Ferguson, Missouri, death of Michael Brown in the summer of 2014. |
| **Reflection**<br>Time: 15 minutes<br><br>Inquiry<br>Community | Students will now have fifteen minutes to report back to the group about what is the meaning of their chosen item as a cultural artifact and why it is important to study it. |
| **Notes:** | Teachers should be sensitive to the cultural milieus of their students and therefore choose items that will have some meaning and weight for the students to examine as they are introduced to the humanities. This is merely an introduction to *why* one does research in the humanities. The introduction to the assignment will be in **Workshop 2: The Assignment.**<br><br>**There is no handout for this workshop. However, the Overview for this workshop can serve as a handout should the teacher wish to give the students a handout.** |

| Common Core Standards: | CCSS.ELA-LITERACY.RH.9-10.1<br>Cite specific textual evidence to support analysis of primary and secondary sources, attending to such features as the date and origin of the information.<br><br>CCSS.ELA-LITERACY.RH.9-10.4<br>Determine the meaning of words and phrases as they are used in a text, including vocabulary describing political, social, or economic aspects of history/social science. |
|---|---|

## Workshop 2

## Overview: The Assignment

The goal of this workshop is the student's review of the assigned humanities research project and its expected outcome of a completed research paper. The review of the assignment in this workshop touches upon all aspects of the research project and the Information Search Process involved in researching a humanities topic. The student is expected to begin brainstorming a topic and browsing for initial information. The assignment introduces students to the following four sections of the paper:

**"Cover Page" with Introduction**
**Body of Paper that Supports the Thesis**
**Conclusion**
**Works Cited**

The humanities research assignment is structured as a scaffolded, piecemeal assignment that can be taught in a cumulative fashion in class meetings, also called workshops. Scaffolding the assignment allows students to budget their work time to accomplish multiple tasks. One-by-one the tasks bring the student researcher to a point in the research project of greater complexity, building knowledge as well as confidence. Much as in real-life problems or projects, a piecemeal approach to the research project makes a large, seemingly difficult task more manageable, and simpler to accomplish for the teenage researcher.

All sections of the paper will be introduced in a workshop format and teachers will guide students through the process. One way of introducing students to the assignment and illustrating the expected product of this research project is to provide examples of already completed papers that portray successful attempts at student research, complete with a research file containing notes and documentation of sources. Such papers do not have to be perfect examples, although they should embody substantive research efforts and clearly demonstrate responsible citations and bibliographic entries. Any student examples should have all names of student authors and any specific identification of the course eliminated in the copy. The copy should be used for classroom use only. Students should not take the sample papers home. While the content of the sample research file and papers may not be perfect, the organization of the paper and the style of presentation should reflect all expectations for an "A" paper so the students can get a good look at a sample of what is expected of them. If such student papers are not available the teacher could create a mock file of research with a mock sample paper.

In this workshop, several elements of the assignment are introduced: the time needed to research, the types of source materials used, intervals of self-assessment, length of research paper, expected style and citation, composition of research folder/notebook, protocols for interrogating sources and note-taking, and expectations for turning in the student's written research report (paper) as well as a possible oral presentation of the research to the class.

## The Vocabulary of Research

The vocabulary of research is often overlooked in high school courses but will be introduced and utilized in this book. Research vocabulary is frequently presented through questions such as:

- What is a student *inquiry*?
- What is a *source*?
- How do you determine its *authenticity*?
- How do you identify its *authority*?
- What is the *timeliness* of the source?
- Are there *oppositional voices* in the source?
- Is it a *primary source*?
- Is it a *secondary source*?
- Is it a *tertiary source*?
- What is the *perspective* of the source?
- Does the source show a *bias*?
- What is a *nontextual source*?
- In what *format* is the source delivered?
- How is the source *presented* (print or digital)?
- Is the *integrity* of the work preserved in the presentation?

Although some students undertaking this project may have conducted humanities research on a smaller scale in earlier grade-level classes, this assignment is intended to introduce or reintroduce a broad, initial mid- to high school-level research project and paper in the humanities. However, it may also be used for a humanities course at the early college level. This project will begin with the student's own inquiry or curiosity about a topic in the humanities that is pertinent to the course, and one in which he will be guided through the research process by a teacher and a librarian to find and choose sources, make notes, organize ideas, and write a report of the research he has undertaken.

All initial research and information handling will be taught and reviewed in a workshop format during class time. Follow-up research will be done at home but then reviewed in the workshop to ensure the student experiences an authentic Information Search Process and produces a humanities research paper.

And finally, to encourage peer-to-peer assistance, support, and student critique, study buddy pairs should be determined by the teacher and announced during the workshop time.

## Workshop 2: The Assignment

**Learning Goals:** The goal of this workshop is an introduction to the Humanities Research Project Assignment.

**Location:** Classroom

**Team:** Teacher and librarian

**Inquiry Unit:** This workshop will provide an introduction to a Guided Inquiry-based humanities research project. The syllabus provides a plan for learning how to do precollegiate scholarship.

**Total Time:** 50 minutes

| **Starter**<br>Time: 15 minutes<br><br>Inquiry<br>Community | Begin the class by displaying on a desk papers from previous years' students. Names of paper authors should not be shown. Ask students about these papers:<br><br>1. Are any topics of interest to you?<br>2. Why were they chosen?<br>3. After looking at a paper can you see the research question being examined?<br>4. Why is this paper called humanities research?<br><br>Teacher will announce study buddy pairs. |
|---|---|
| **Work Time**<br>Time: 30 minutes<br><br>Inquiry<br>Community | Provide the students with the workshop **Handouts #1, #2, and #3**. Ask individual students to read segments of the handouts. Focus on the different sections of the assignment and the different expectations for completion.<br>　　The second half of the work time will be spent discussing the Information Search Process. See figure 1.1 in the *Teacher's Practicum*, which may be copied and given to the students or projected on the whiteboard. The librarian will take the students verbally through the seven stages of the Information Search Process as it relates to their research. |
| **Reflection**<br>Time: 5 minutes<br><br>Inquiry<br>Community | Each workshop has a time for brief reflection either for the whole class or between study buddies. Questions to reflect upon:<br><br>1. Is this assignment comprehensible?<br>2. What is unclear about the assignment?<br>3. How do I feel about the assignment? |

| Notes: | The twenty workshops described in this book can be done by students in print format, digitally, or both. The print book itself is held by each student, providing ample space for additional manual note-taking and also serving as a workbook for student handouts. |
|---|---|
| | This workshop is complex. The teacher and librarian (guides) and students may need a second workshop period to completely answer student questions. |
| | **Throughout this curriculum, extra workshop time is frequently suggested as unstructured workshops so that students may complete the work and not fall behind. Additionally, the unstructured workshop time allows the teacher and librarian more capability for observation and hands-on intervention. Therefore, please thoroughly read these workshops before scheduling the workshop times.** |
| **Common Core Standards:** | CCSS.ELA-LITERACY.SL.9-10.1<br>Initiate and participate effectively in a range of collaborative discussions (one-on-one, in groups, and teacher-led) with diverse partners on grades 9–10 topics, texts, and issues, building on others' ideas and expressing their own clearly and persuasively.<br><br>CCSS.ELA-LITERACY.WHST.9-10.7<br>Conduct short as well as more sustained research projects to answer a question (including a self-generated question) or solve a problem; narrow or broaden the inquiry when appropriate; synthesize multiple sources on the subject, demonstrating understanding of the subject under investigation.<br><br>CCSS.ELA-LITERACY.W.9-10.6<br>Use technology, including the Internet, to produce, publish, and update individual or shared writing products, taking advantage of technology's capacity to link to other information and to display information flexibly and dynamically. |

# Workshop 2

## *Student Handout #1: Borrowing Information: The Big Idea Behind Research*

A person does not begin a research project unless he needs to know something. If he already knows that something then presumably there is no need to embark on a research project.

Until recently, most high school and early collegiate research projects were conducted by students who were informed by their teachers about the strict parameters involved. The students were given a list (short or long) of possible topics and a list of types of sources and desired outcomes. For example:

A research paper on Mark Twain might have used five different sources including one work of Twain's fiction, one biography, and three different cultural essay analyses of the featured Twain work. The paper was expected to contain a thesis, three evidential examples or "proofs" of the thesis from the sources, and a thoughtful conclusion by the student researcher. The paper was expected to be five to ten pages long and would include a bibliography for all properly cited works.

Now, however, with the adoption of inquiry-based learning curricula, research projects are becoming much more student-generated. Sources are also becoming broader, deeper, and more dispersed as the digital environment explodes. One thing remains constant: *the research project is conducted to satisfy a need to know*. While the need to know is now more often based upon a student's individual choice of subject or even the student's more personalized question, the research project still stands as a method of "borrowing" information to answer a question and to satisfy the student's need to know.

The big idea behind the act of doing research, therefore, remains the same as it has through the centuries. That big idea is to borrow information from sources—and people who are the sources. Those sources may provide the student researcher with some of what is known about the topic/question. The researcher takes the information by borrowing it and stating that he has borrowed it, as he quotes, paraphrases, or summarizes the information and cites the source.

To develop his paper the student researcher includes as much borrowed information as he chooses (and/or has been required) in his notes and in his written research report. The beauty and creativity of borrowing information is that the student researcher chooses to borrow only what is meaningful to him. The combination of sources of borrowed information is also unique to him and that combination, joined with the student's prior knowledge and understanding of the research subject material, will usually instigate and initiate newer thoughts and new, deeper understanding of the research subject matter.

Suddenly the borrowed information has become fertile soil for the student's own ideas and unique personalized understanding. He begins to "own" his research topic.

### Important Note to the Student Researcher

However, students should be constantly reminded to be truthful and accurate about the borrowed information. There is no dishonor in using borrowed intellectual property of others. That is really the essence and the big idea behind doing research. If you attempt to answer a question or questions that you cannot answer with the knowledge that you have in your head, then of course you must borrow information from other sources to help yourself formulate ideas about the research question. That borrowed information is not your own intellectual property but it belongs to someone else—to another source—usually to another person or persons.

Usually the more sources you have, the more sources you use. The more information you gather and borrow from the source, the more you learn. You then gain a broader and deeper understanding of the research topic.

*All* of the information you borrow must be indicated in a text citation and listed in a bibliography on a works cited page. Only then are you truthfully accounting for your research and only then are you telling the reader or observer where you got the old borrowed information.

There is **great dishonor and fraud in not acknowledging borrowed information** and in pretending to either be the source of the information yourself or pretending to not know where that borrowed information came from. **Underlying such fraud is a lack of scholarly humility.** Authentic scholars know that without true research and without borrowing information passed down from one age or era to another, human knowledge will not progress. If people learn from each other and borrow what they learn, new ideas and new knowledge become possible. This is the big idea behind research and scholarship.

## Workshop 2

### *Student Handout #2: Sample Assignment of a Humanities Research Paper*

You are now beginning to research and write a humanities research paper about the work of some person, a movement, a historical feature, or social/political factor and its influence on the culture of the United States of America. Your paper will focus on the cultural work itself, not on the biography of the individual involved. Your research should include critical commentary about the work.

Class will meet 2–3 times per week for several weeks in the library to generate topics, find source materials, and conduct the research. Other class times may be announced for library research workshops. Among your assignments are:

*Topic Approved*                                   Due Date_____

A separate 1" three ring binder with **Parent Signature Due** [*] **(keep one copy of schedule at home, one copy in your binder and hand in one copy). Failure to hand this in on time will result in a loss of 5 points off the final grade average. If you are absent, fax it to school or have someone deliver it.**

*Five Sources Due* (5 points)                      Due Date_____

**The sources must be physically brought to class on this date.** We want to be sure that you have sufficient material to proceed. Encyclopedias do not count here, although they may be one of the eight sources required. *General Internet material is not to be used either, but academic databases may be used.* A good distribution of sources at this time would be: works by the person, primary sources (letters, documents, news articles, journals), secondary sources including at least three critical and scholarly sources about your subject, historical source material, news articles, or videos and a biography or autobiography (if appropriate).

*Initial Notes Due* (20 points)                    Due Date_____

**Minimum of 10 full typed pages or the equivalent of approximately 5–10 notecards per page or 50–100 handwritten or typed note cards** in your notebook with source and page numbers clearly labeled. Record all information accurately. Label each note as a direct quotation, paraphrase, or summary. (Use quotation marks in the quote notes.) If you have your own unique note system show the librarian and we will negotiate.

*Formulated Research Question* (5 points)          Due Date_____

This is an ongoing discussion that we will have together; it is possible that in the course of researching you may want to modify your initial question.

---

[*] If the assignment is for a college course, the signature due is the student's signature.

*Last Sources Due* (5 points)                    Due Date_____

This date may be adjusted if last minute changes are needed.

*Final Notes Due* (20 points)                    Due Date_____

Here you will need at least 50–100 more notes. This date for notecards may be adjusted if last minute changes are needed. **The notes should be typed and the same guidelines used as above in the initial notes.** These notes are **in addition** to the initial 10 pages of notes. The information needs to be sufficient to support your thesis.

*Thesis Approved* (5 points)                    Due Date_____

*Outline Due* (20 points)                    Due Date_____

*First Draft Due* (20 points)                    Due Date_____

**Typed with parenthetical citations and bibliography.** During this time there will be an opportunity for peer review of the first draft.

*Final Paper* (100 points)                    Due Date_____

All materials produced, collected, and evaluated must also be handed in with the final paper including all notes, outlines, and drafts. If any portion of the graded materials is not in your research binder, the final paper will not be accepted, and you will receive only the points accumulated before "final paper due."

\* Three self-assessments are scheduled for this project, at the beginning, middle, and end of the project. These assessments, known as the SLIM packet, will provide extra credit of 7 points per assessment for those students who complete them. **The SLIM packet can be found in the appendix.**

Adapted from the Gill St. Bernard's English Department
Tenth-Grade Research Paper Schedule

# Workshop 2

## *Student Handout #3: Parts of Your Humanities Paper*

I.   **"Cover Page" with the introduction is the first page of your research paper and contains:**

   a.   *The Heading*

   Full name

   Teacher's name

   Class name

   Date paper is turned in

   b.   *Introduction*

   A statement that opens with a hook to grab the attention of the reader and then indicates a thesis based upon supporting evidence you found while pursuing a research question that supports your basic thesis.

II.  **Body of Paper**

   Three examples of detailed content or evidence that support (or challenge) your thesis statement.

   a)   Each example is sometimes called a proof. Each example is several paragraphs long and gives an organized body of evidence (several statements or indications) about a key point that illustrates and provides details to explain the thesis statement.

   b)   Each example or supporting evidence is focused on one key aspect.

III. **Conclusion**

   A concluding two or more paragraphs that are not identical to the introduction but instead provide a crafted assessment, without adding new material, of the relationships between the thesis and the supporting bodies of evidence for the thesis. The conclusion should answer the question, what does all this research mean? You may also indicate where future research should be directed.

IV.  **Works Cited**

   Here, in MLA Style, is a complete listing of each and every source borrowed and used.

# Workshop 3

## Overview: Encouraging a Variety of Sources and Formats

The goal of this workshop is the students' understanding of a need for and use of different types of sources and formats for newly borrowed information. When a student receives a research project assignment he is often dismayed to learn that several different sources are required for research. And if the assignment calls for different formats in which those sources are presented, confusion may reign. The student may wonder, "What is a source and what is a format, and how do these two things relate to my paper?"

For most students, this assignment is not the first time the teacher has required more than one source of information. But perhaps the student has never learned the principle of multiple sources of information in conducting a research project. For research purposes three types of sources exist: first person (primary), second person (secondary), or third person (tertiary).

A source of information in the humanities is usually some written or spoken work or made object which can be one of three levels of "closeness" to the subject being studied. The work or object can be a **primary or first person source**, which comes directly from contact with the topic being studied. The work or object can be a **secondary or second person source**, which comes from the effort of someone who interacted with the first person source about the subject and then created a work or object using his own interpretation of the subject being studied. And finally, a source of a work or object may be a **tertiary or third person source**, which was created after interacting with secondary (second person) sources of the subject being studied.

Each of these three types of sources is different in that each will portray the subject being studied in a partial way. The primary source will be affected by his direct experience of the event with his own perspective. The secondary source's portrayal of the subject will be affected by his distance in time and place from the event, as well as his choice of primary source(s) of the event and his own interpretation of those source(s). In other words, unlike the primary source that does not have to borrow any information to discuss and create his story for the subject, the secondary source must borrow information from the primary source or sources to create his story of the subject being studied. Therefore, if the secondary source used more than one primary source, the student researcher may get a fuller, more accurate, and more nuanced picture of the subject he is researching. And that is essentially why multiple sources of information are encouraged when a subject is being researched.

A tertiary source of research is one that uses mainly secondary sources to obtain information. Thus, a tertiary source may have a fuller, broader picture of the subject but because that source relies on secondary sources of borrowed information, the secondary sources are once removed from the subject, carry re-interpretations, and have secondary source biases about the research subject. Therefore, a tertiary source will have at least two sets of biases and may have dozens of different kinds of source materials.

## Different Kinds of Source Materials

Among those three types of sources, the researcher can also find all kinds of source materials, including both textual and nontextual information sources, which may be held in three-dimensional objects such as books or artifacts as well as digitally accessed through devices.

Another frequent requirement of a researcher is the use of multiple formats of information as well as multiple sources. A format of information is how the information is packaged for delivery to the user of the information. Let us use the example of a piece of music that is being borrowed by the researcher. The piece, "We Are One (Ole Ola)," is a song sung by Jennifer Lopez along with two others singers, Claudia Leitte and Pitbull. They sang this song in Brazil in July, 2014 at a World Cup soccer game. The song, written by Armando C. Perez, Thomas Troelsen, Jennifer Lopez, and others, may be found in several formats. One format would be a printed version of the sheet music from the original composers. Another format could be a recording made by the television network that produced the 2014 World Cup. A third format could be a posting on YouTube by someone who surreptitiously filmed Jennifer Lopez singing the song. As the students may now understand, the type of format the information is packaged in will affect the manner in which the information is received by the researcher and even how it is borrowed by him for the project.

## Oppositional Voices

The necessity of using multiple and varied sources and formats is underscored by the researcher's experience encountering oppositional voices while interacting with different sources. Oppositional voices is a term for content that disagrees with other content, each voice providing possibly conflicting evidence with the other. Indeed, this is the essence of scholarship and of scholarly thinking: to search for, find, and sift through a variety of voices, concepts, biases, perspectives, and information, and to think about and analyze all that is encountered, especially if what is encountered on one hand is opposed to that which is encountered on the other hand. Oppositional voices in research sources often require further research for the scholar as he continues to interpret and more deeply understand the subject being studied. An extraordinary English teacher at Gill St. Bernard's School, Derek Martin, once said, "In terms of credibility, whether in medicine or the humanities, a second opinion is a good thing."

## Cultural Perspectives

To encourage a variety of sources and formats, the humanities in modern times should also be studied with the understanding that the researcher will encounter many voices within a wide array of cultural perspectives. Cultural perspectives are the points of view influenced by different aspects of culture that the writer or producer of the information has lived or has valued. Aspects of culture include age, race, gender, religion, geographic location, socioeconomic position (class), history, scientific position, and cognitive stance. Some of these cultural aspects may be incorporated into the information produced by the source being used, and thus should be understood as lending cultural perspective(s) to the information producer.

## Workshop 3: Encouraging a Variety of Sources and Formats

**Learning Goals:** The goal of this workshop is to explain the need for and encourage the use of a variety of sources in different formats.

**Location:** Library

**Team:** Teacher, librarian, and resource guide

**Inquiry Unit:** This workshop establishes the function of sources to provide information and to explore the use of a variety of sources and formats to ensure a broader research information base.

**Total Time:** 50 minutes

| | |
|---|---|
| **Starter**<br>Time: 15 minutes<br><br>Inquiry<br>Community | As the class gathers, play a song from a recent concert such as Beyoncé and Jay-Z or an old song by the Beatles. Ask the class to identify the song and explore who wrote it, who performed it, and the kind of format in which the song was delivered.<br><br>The librarian presents ten or more vessels holding information: a book, an artwork, a newspaper, a tablet, a CD, a baseball glove, a DVD of a movie, etc. The librarian distributes and reviews **Handout #1: List of Resources for a Humanities Research Paper (Sample)**. |
| **Work Time**<br>Time: 25 minutes<br><br>Study Buddies | The class breaks up into groups of study buddies and each pair chooses one humanities artifact, a photo, a piece of art, a movie, a musical piece, etc., and returns to the workshop community to discuss the piece. Ask the following:<br><br>Is it a first, second, or third person source?<br>How is the source held? That is, what kind of vessel or container holds the information?<br>In what format?<br><br>Using an example of recent editorials in the newspaper, ask the students to identify at least one set (2) of oppositional voices as they are conducting their research. Ask them how the voices (or sources) oppose or disagree with one another. Finally, ask the students to try to identify a cultural perspective of a main source of information they may have already encountered. |
| **Reflection**<br>Time: 10 minutes<br><br>Inquiry<br>Community | During the reflection time, ask for volunteers who will explain different sources and artifacts, the nature of the artifact, what information may be taken from the artifact, and how the artifact might surprise the researcher. |
| **Notes:** | This is not the last of the discussions about sources but rather an introduction. Other workshops such as **Workshop 7: Research in the Ubiquitous Media Environment, Workshop 8: Searching for Humanities Sources**, and **Workshop 13: Interrogating the Sources** will also focus on the nature of resources for the humanities and what to do with those sources. |

| Common Core Standards: | CCSS.ELA-LITERACY.RL.9-10.7<br>Analyze the representation of a subject or a key scene in two different artistic mediums, including what is emphasized or absent in each treatment (e.g., Auden's "Musée des Beaux Arts" and Breughel's "Landscape with the Fall of Icarus").<br><br>CCSS.ELA-LITERACY.RH.9-10.9<br>Compare and contrast treatments of the same topic in several primary and secondary sources. |
|---|---|

# Workshop 3

## *Student Handout #1: List of Resources for a Humanities Research Paper (Sample)*

The library provides access to a number of different kinds of resources, which you can use for your research. Some types of sources will be more useful depending on your topic. The information below will provide you with some guidelines that will get you started.

If you have chosen the work of a person, an excellent way to start is to read a short biography (1–2 pages), either in a database or in a biographical encyclopedia or critical essay. This allows you to get a sense of who, when, and perhaps why the person created what he did.

**If you have chosen an author:** Some of the databases we subscribe to will be very helpful. These include Literature Resource Center (part of Infotrac database), Literature Reference Center (part of Ebscohost), World of Poetry Online, Bloom's Literary Reference Online (part of Facts on File database), and JSTOR. Depending on the author, the library may have books written by the author or books of criticism. In the reference room there may be volumes of *Literary Criticism* and *Literature and Its Time*. Interlibrary loans can be used to obtain books from other libraries.

**If you have chosen an artist, photographer, or architect:** The library has an extensive art book collection. These will allow you to see what the work looks like. The books can also provide criticism, *often in the forward or introduction*. In the reference room is a set of books, *Modern Arts Criticism*, that will be helpful for some students. Some of the databases that will be helpful include Gale Virtual Reference Library (electronic versions of many reference books), Proquest/New York Times, Ebsco Master File, and ELibrary.

**If you have chosen a historic movement and its influence about history:** A good way to start is to read a short overview (1–3 pages) of the period. The library has books that will be helpful. Destiny, the library online catalog, can be used to search our holdings. Databases will also be helpful. Speak with one of the librarians to find what will work best for your topic.

Information about how to access the databases, including URLs, usernames, and passwords is available on the Knightsite. This document is in the Library Services section which is in Knightfiles.

If you need assistance finding sources, the librarians are always available to help.

Claudia Hesler, Assistant Librarian, Gill St. Bernard's School, 2014

## Workshop 4

## Overview: Hunting for Information and Browsing for Ideas

The first time the student goes to the library to research his topic he should be allowed to randomly hunt for information, that is, to browse for ideas. From the time the teacher initially mentions the assignment, until the time the student goes to the library, he may have thought about a topic or he may not have thought at all!

When the student enters the library he may not be aware that this is his information nirvana where he will find the librarians, the collection, the databases, and help guides. If the student has a possible topic in mind, in the first thirty to forty minutes he will look through some materials such as specialized encyclopedias, books, pictures, the online catalog of library holdings, or on the internet.

Perhaps he originally comes to the library to look for one topic. In handling the first sources of material the student's interest may shift to an ancillary topic or subtopic about which he knows little. If that occurs he must hunt for more information; this is almost a process of elimination of the possible topics. The student must browse enough to find the topic that most piques his interest, which becomes the possible subject of his new research. If the hunt is not successful, more library time should be scheduled during and/or after class while a teacher or librarian is still available. **See Handout 1: Two Paths and Seven Steps in Hunting for Information and Browsing for Ideas.**

Hunting for information is not a smooth process; it is somewhat like searching for something in the dark. Each step of the hunt may not mean progress. The student who is searching will hit a dead end with no information or may bump into a wall of information so large it appears impenetrable. Librarians can help a student search by suggesting, although not retrieving, some varied resources for possible topics. Taking the student to the location of the sources the librarian will, perhaps, show the student specialized encyclopedias, or photographic compendiums about the topic, play some music or pull out full-color print recipe books about a geographic region the student is interested in. All of these are examples of small help by the guides. What the teacher and librarian should avoid is sitting down to a computer with the student beside him and printing out all the necessary articles. On the other hand, discussing initial online search strategies with a student who has chosen to research first online is acceptable. The point is to get the student to do the searching. See **Handout 2: Databases for the Humanities Research Paper (Sample).**

Most teachers, when designing an original assignment, will indicate a number of sources and require a variety of those sources. Teachers who are familiar with student browsing behavior know that at first the student may just be browsing for an idea and only after that will begin actually studying or interacting with the materials and possible research sources. When we include hunting for information, what we are saying to students is: come into the library, look at some physical and digital sources, and by inspiration, the process of elimination, or just plain luck in your browsing, you will get some ideas about your possible research topic.

## Workshop 4: Hunting for Information and Browsing for Ideas

**Learning Goals:** The goal of this workshop is the student's initial foray into library research and his understanding that his first efforts might not go smoothly, although help is available to him.

**Location:** Library

**Team:** Teacher, librarian, and resource guide

**Inquiry Unit:** The student's inquiry is how to start the research project by investigating initial sources.

**Total Time:** 50 minutes

| Starter<br>Time: 15 minutes<br><br>Inquiry<br>Community | As the class gathers in the reference area of the library, students are asked to put backpacks away as they begin their mission to hunt for information and get some ideas about a possible research topic. **Handout #1: Two Paths and Seven Steps in Hunting for Information and Browsing for Ideas** is read to the whole class and the two paths are discussed. Each student is also given **Handout #2: Databases for the Humanities Research Papers** to look at and possibly use at this time. The librarian may display some possible first sources to look at including specialized encyclopedias that are simply used for initial reference. **Handout #3: Interrogating a Nonfiction Text (Encyclopedia)** should be distributed and will be useful. |
|---|---|
| **Work Time**<br>Time: 30 minutes<br><br>Individual<br>Scholars | Students may go individually to a section of the library and begin to browse. The librarian, teacher, and resource guide should individually consult with each student while the students are browsing and be available if the student needs help. |
| **Reflection**<br>Time: 5 minutes<br><br>Inquiry<br>Community | Students should congregate as a class and discuss:<br><br>1. How did their searching go?<br>2. How are they feeling?<br>3. What happens next? |
| **Notes:** | Three handouts have been prepared for this workshop. None of these handouts is exhaustive, but each provides the neophyte humanities researcher with some place to begin browsing, looking for and at sources. Very little note-taking is going on at this point. Students who are still not finished browsing should continue to do so on their own time unless the teacher chooses to allow another one or two unstructured workshop times to permit more browsing. Extra time will allow for students to become more familiar with the library environment and the access to numerous resources. **We highly recommend this extra time!** |

| Common Core Standards: | CCSS.ELA-LITERACY.WHST.9-10.8<br>Gather relevant information from multiple authoritative print and digital sources, using advanced searches effectively; assess the usefulness of each source in answering the research question; integrate information into the text selectively to maintain the flow of ideas, avoiding plagiarism and following a standard format for citation.<br><br>CCSS.ELA-LITERACY.RI.9-10.8<br>Delineate and evaluate the argument and specific claims in a text, assessing whether the reasoning is valid and the evidence is relevant and sufficient; identify false statements and fallacious reasoning. |
|---|---|

# Workshop 4

## *Handout #1: Two Paths and Seven Steps in Hunting for Information and Browsing for Ideas*

As a new humanities researcher you should realize that coming up with a research topic that you get excited about, can live with, and keep working on for the next eight to ten weeks is not going to be an easy task. Below you will find two different paths, each with seven steps to lead you on your information search journey.

### Path One: For someone who thinks he knows his topic:

A.  First, look at reference materials in print or online that deal with your topic:

   1.  Specialized encyclopedias

   2.  Guides or handbooks

   3.  Anthologies or compendiums

B.  Then look at library holdings:

   4.  Online catalog

   5.  Go to shelves and look in the area of the subfield of knowledge about your topic

C.  Expand your search to include:

   6.  Online databases

   7.  Talk with a librarian or content expert for guidance

### Path Two: For someone who has no idea what his topic may be:

A.  Pique your interest:

   1.  Look at the magazine racks for possible subject matter.

   2.  Think about the things you like to learn about, especially considering your learning style, and make a list of those things.

B.  Talk to someone who can help you with the possibilities:

   3.  Librarian

   4.  Teacher or content expert

C.  After that look at Path One above:

   5.  Look at letter A

   6.  Look at letter B

   7.  Look at letter C

## Workshop 4

### *Student Handout #2: Databases for the Humanities Research Paper (Sample)*

The library subscribes to a number of different databases. For your research, the ones that will be most helpful are listed below. The easiest way to access the databases is to go the school's website. This document is in the Library Services section, which is in "Knightfiles." If you need assistance the librarians are available to help.

**Literature Resource Center:** Biographical information, criticism, works' overviews, and more.
URL: http://infotrac.galegroup.com/itweb/gillsb_ca
**From school:** username and password are not needed.
**From home:**
Username:
Password:

**Literature Reference Center (part of EBSCO):** Similar to the above database but uses different sources.
URL: http://search.ebscohost.com
**From school:** username and password are not needed.
**From home:**
Username:
Password:

**World of Poetry Online:** Full text poetry linked to commentaries and criticism.
URL: http://www.columbiagrangers.org/grangers/
**From school:** username and password are not needed.
**From home:**
Username:
Password:

**Bloom's Literary Reference Online (part of Facts on File):** The critic Harold Bloom's and other authors' literary criticism, overviews, and analyses.
URL: http://www.fofweb.com/subscription
**From school:** username and password are not needed.
**From home:**
Username:
Password:

**Gale Virtual Reference Library:** Electronic versions of many reference books. It includes the *Encyclopedia of World Biography* and many literature reference titles.
URL: http://infotrac.galegroup.com/itweb/gillsb_ca
**From school:** username and password are not needed.
**From home:**
Username:
Password:

**Proquest/New York Times:** Searches over 2,000 periodicals, the *New York Times*, and eight other newspapers.
 URL: http://portal.bigchalk.com/portalweb/home.do
 **From school:** username and password are not needed.
 **From home:**
 Username:
 Password:


**Master File (part of EBSCO):** Searches 2,000 periodicals; some overlap with Proquest.
 URL: http://search.ebscohost.com
 **From school:** username and password are not needed.
 Username:
 Password:


**ELibrary:** Searches magazines, newspapers, books, and TV and radio transcripts.
 URL: http://portal.bigchalk.com/portalweb/home.do
 **From school:** username and password are not needed.
 **From home:**
 Username:
 Password:

Claudia Hesler, Assistant Librarian, Gill St. Bernard's School, 2014

## Workshop 4

### *Student Handout #3: Interrogating a Nonfiction Text That Is an Encyclopedia (General or Specialized)*

There are several different types of nonfiction texts and your use of them depends on your stage of research. At the beginning of a research task you are looking for an overview of your topic, not too complicated, in which to immerse yourself. You have a choice at this stage between print and electronic versions of a simple nonfiction text, such as a general or specialized encyclopedia. **Your focus is the broad picture because you need to get a sense of your topic as a whole.**

Later in your research, when you have formed the focus you want to follow, you will be looking for deeper and more pertinent information. You will then need a different type of nonfiction text.

### Interrogating an Encyclopedia Article

**Before you begin to read the article, think about:**

1. What do I already know about this topic?
2. What am I interested in finding out about this topic?
3. What questions do I have that this article might answer?
4. Do I need to focus closely on the whole article? Are there sections I can leave out?
5. What does the layout of the article tell me about the topic?
6. What do the headings and subheadings tell me about the topic?
7. What do pictures, charts, and weblinks (if an online encyclopedia) tell me about the topic?

**During your reading of the article think about:**

1. What answers does this article have for my questions?
2. What does the introduction tell me?
3. Can I distill the content of this article into two or three sentences?
4. Are there pictures, charts, multimedia, and other linked content, or a reference list that could inform me more clearly of the content and send me to some sources for my research?
5. Does the article force me to ask new questions?
6. What are those questions?

**After you read the article, ask yourself:**

1. Am I still interested in the topic?

2. What have I learned from reading this article?

3. How will I record what I learned? Shall I make a graphic organizer, use notecards, or use a digital note-taking program?

4. What further questions do I now have to direct my research?

5. What interests me about this topic?

6. What search terms are emerging for me as I read about this topic?

**Remember: When you are reading an encyclopedia or any other overview, keep your notes VERY brief. You are looking for the broad brush, the context of your topic. Do not go into great detail at this early stage of your research, because it may confuse you. You do not need to record bibliographic details for an encyclopedia.** *YOU WILL NOT* **USE THIS SPECIALIZED OR GENERAL ENCYCLOPEDIA ARTICLE FOR ONE OF YOUR SOURCES.**

Lee Fitzgerald, Charles Sturt College, Australia

## Research in the Selection Stage of the Information Search Process

Workshop 5: Coming Up with a Topic and Beginning to Ask a Question
Workshop 6: What Is Culture and What Is Cultural Criticism?
Workshop 7: Research in the Ubiquitous Media Environment
Workshop 8: Searching for Humanities Sources
Workshop 9: The Research Question

During the Selection Stage, five workshops are scheduled and detailed herein. At this stage students are tentatively deciding upon a topic that will become central to the need for information sources and the cultural criticism that students learn about in the workshops. The student will begin searching and handling initial materials during the structured workshops. Other nonstructured workshops will provide students with time to look for and interact with initial sources. Both librarian and teacher should be available for one-on-one conferencing with individual students. Students should be reminded that the teacher and librarian are their information search process guides and are here to help.

During Selection, optimism is displayed as students choose a topic they wish to investigate. If, however, some students do not display such optimism the librarian should intervene and offer assistance.

# Workshop 5

## Overview: Coming Up with a Topic and Beginning to Ask a Question

The goal of this workshop is for the student to tentatively decide upon a research topic after he has browsed through different sources for topic ideas. A secondary goal is for the student to initially phrase his research subject as a simple question that he will ask his sources to help him answer. Because the neophyte researcher has very little intellectual capital (prior accurate knowledge) about his research subject, framing a research question or even choosing a scholarly research topic in the humanities will take some effort.

So let us begin. The roles of the teacher and librarian at this point are to be encouraging guides. If the student suggests a topic that is new to you or seems unusual, a research interview in a nonthreatening or critical way with the student may be in order. Questions to ask the student include:

- Why are you interested in your suggested topic?
- What do you already know about this topic?
- When did you first encounter the topic?
- How do you best learn? Can you describe your learning style?
- Do you think your learning style will help you to conduct several hours of research and note-taking about this topic?
- What formats of information will you use to conduct your research?
- Do you know of any primary sources about your research topic?
- What is one question you have about the topic that is fresh in your mind and that you would like to have answered?

All these questions will appear on student **Handout #1: What Is Your Topic?** for this workshop. The ISP guides (teacher, librarian, and any other aide) should avoid providing topics to the student. Student choice of topic is a cornerstone of the Guided Inquiry approach to humanities research. Responsibility for the choice of topic should remain with the student.

However, within the freedom of topical choice there is a responsibility to focus on the field or subfield of knowledge being taught in the course. If the humanities research project takes place in an American history course, then the parameters of choice of topic are set in the American history subfield. Other parameters may include time, history, issue, or movement. The same type of responsibilities may also limit a literature or art humanities research project as well.

While it is acceptable to provide students with examples of past research projects, teachers should refrain from providing a shopping list of suggested topics and requiring students to choose a topic from that list, as this does not fulfill the objective of student choice of topic.

At times the teacher or librarian guide will encounter a student who is at a loss and cannot come up with a research topic. In our experience at least one or two students in each class initially display this inability. For the student's sake such a student may need extra time and more guidance in choosing a topic. Perhaps he is intimidated by the project and the work it entails. Perhaps his learning style does not lend itself to a traditional research paper. Perhaps the student is simply indifferent to academics. All these reasons call for a more personalized approach to the research assignment and to the student's understanding of the responsibilities he must fulfill.

Referring to the diagram of the Information Search Process on page 7 the teacher and librarian can recognize the affective behaviors exhibited throughout the research project. These behaviors may not manifest at the same time for each student. At the end of the Initiation Stage and the beginning of the Selection Stage of the project, a student may still feel uncertain about his topic, and his uncertainty increases because he cannot make a decision about a possible topic while others are selecting topics. At this time the teacher or librarian guide should sit down with the uncertain student, and conduct a caring and careful interview in a quiet and private space.

Among the questions to ask the student are:

- How are you feeling about this assignment?
- What is it that you do not like about the assignment?
- Have you ever done formal or informal research that you enjoyed?
- What was that research about?
- Why was that research enjoyable?
- What do you not like about research?
- Would you feel better if you knew that a teacher would help you with the difficult parts?
- If you could choose any topic to learn about, what would it be?
- What is your favorite academic or nonacademic activity and why?
- What is your favorite class and why?
- Can you connect any aspect of your favorite class or activity to something you would want to research?
- Because research can be conducted with film, video, interviews, music, sports, etc., what kinds of sources interest you other than books or online text?
- Would you like to see some past papers on subjects that interest you?
- Would it help to have a study buddy or peer reviewer, someone from this class who can lend you some help or who you can brainstorm with?

After the interview with the student is completed, a better picture will emerge for the teacher or librarian about the reluctant student researcher. The student himself may gain a more positive picture of his instructor guides and of the research process itself.

## Workshop 5: Coming Up with a Topic and Beginning to Ask a Question

**Learning Goals:** The goal of this workshop is the student's selection of a possible research topic and an initial effort to ask a research question.

**Location:** Library

**Team:** Teacher, librarian, and resource guide

**Inquiry Unit:** This stage of inquiry incorporates student choice of topic and begins to explore the topic through the articulation of a simple research question.

**Total Time:** 50 minutes

| | |
|---|---|
| **Starter**<br>Time: 15 minutes<br><br>Inquiry<br>Community | The teacher opens the class period with an anecdote about his own early research experience that did not go smoothly, or he may ask students to relate similar stories about past research. The librarian can then explain that in the process of selecting a topic some basic questions may help to begin the research. The teacher gives students **Handout #1: What Is Your Topic?** Then the librarian, with several print examples in hand, will discuss how using a specialized encyclopedia or other reference guides might help with a topic choice. **Handout #3: Interrogating a Nonfiction Text That Is an Encyclopedia** from **Workshop 4: Hunting for Information and Browsing for Ideas** can also be used here again. |
| **Work Time**<br>Time: 30 minutes<br><br>Individual<br>Scholars | Using the two handouts, students are asked to begin looking at possible sources in the reference room, including both print and digital reference works to determine a possible topic. |
| **Reflection**<br>Time: 5 minutes<br><br>Study Buddies | During the last few minutes of the workshop, the student should discuss possible questions he thought of with his assigned study buddy. |
| **Notes:** | The next workshop will examine the concept and examples of cultural criticism. Prior to that workshop students may need more unstructured workshop time to choose a topic.<br><br>During the unstructured time, the teacher and librarian circulate to discuss research options with each student. The resource guide will be available to help the most reticent researcher(s) choose a topic. |

| Common Core Standards: | CCSS.ELA-LITERACY.W.9-10.1.A<br>Introduce precise claim(s), distinguish the claim(s) from alternate or opposing claims, and create an organization that establishes clear relationships among claim(s), counterclaims, reasons, and evidence.<br><br>CCSS.ELA-LITERACY.W.9-10.2.A<br>Introduce a topic; organize complex ideas, concepts, and information to make important connections and distinctions; include formatting (e.g., headings), graphics (e.g., figures, tables), and multimedia when useful to aiding comprehension. |
|---|---|

# Workshop 5

## *Student Handout #1: What Is Your Topic?*

Why are you interested in your suggested topic?

What do you already know about this topic?

When did you first encounter the topic?

What is one question you have about the topic that is fresh in your mind and that you would like to have answered?

How do you best learn? Can you describe your learning style?

Do you think your learning style will help you to conduct several hours of research and note-taking about this topic?

What formats of information will you use to conduct your research?

Do you know of any primary sources about your research topic?

## Workshop 6

## Overview: What Is Culture and What Is Cultural Criticism?

The goal of this workshop is to introduce students to the concept of cultural criticism and the role that cultural criticism plays in interpreting and understanding the humanities, both in public life and the academic arena.

In the latter half of the twentieth century, the political theorist Hannah Arendt described three types of human activity: *Labor*, which she said humans accomplished to meet basic survival needs of food, protection, and continuation; *Work*, which she said was the activity of fabricating the implements and tools of human existence; *Action*, which she said creates the new beginnings that sustain and push forward humanity (Arendt, 1998, 7). Below is a brief excerpt from Arendt's second edition of the *The Human Condition* delineating these ideas.

> . . . in man, otherness which he shares with everything that is, and distinctness, which he shares with everything alive, become uniqueness, and human plurality is the paradoxical plurality of unique beings.
>
> Speech and action reveal this unique distinctness. Through them, men distinguish themselves instead of being merely distinct; they are the modes in which human beings appear to each other, not indeed as physical objects, but qua men. This appearance, as distinguished from mere bodily existence, rests on initiative but it is an initiative from which no human being can refrain and still be human . . .
>
> With word and deed we insert ourselves into the human world and this insertion is a second birth, in which we confirm and take upon ourselves the naked fact of our original physical appearance. This insertion is not forced upon us by necessity, like labor, and it is not prompted by utility like work. (176)

For Hannah Arendt, human speech and action equate with the creativity that connects individual humans to the ongoing story of humanity and, in fact, advances that story. This definition can be used to describe and define human culture. Human culture is manifest in the creation of words and actions connecting one human's initiative with the ongoing story of humanity. This is the activity of culture. Culture, in Arendt's definition, is that which is produced by humans above and beyond the production of labor that satisfies basic human necessities of survival, and work that produces the tools and instruments to ease the labor of survival. Speech and action as differentiated from labor and work create new beginnings and new definitions of the human enterprise and thus allow humans to go forward into time and space (Arendt, 1998, 178).

Culture is then the result of creative effort. It can be an object, an activity, an idea, a movement, or an organization of effort. Culture is that which the artist or creator (originator) of some new beginning makes to break the commonly known layer of human existence. The new beginning may initiate a new understanding of what lies ahead in human history (such as Abraham Lincoln's speech, *The Gettysburg Address*) or may provide a new path to human communication (such as the jazz musical works of saxophonist Charlie "Bird" Parker), or it may encapsulate a new definition of beauty (such as Van Gogh's *Irises*). Whatever the cultural work is, it leaves humanity with something new to think about, redefining the boundaries of human existence.

A humanities paper examines some aspect or aspects of culture that humans have created, either through history, art, politics, or other iterations of human speaking and acting beyond their basic modes of labor and work. Culture constitutes the activities and creations that set us apart as humans from the other species and permit us to reinterpret or understand in a different light what the act of living is all about.

The humanities research paper that the student is undertaking reflects the student's choice to study some aspect of human culture. And precisely because the student knows little about the chosen subject, some of his first forays into an information search, after first identifying his subject, should be to examine what cultural critics have said about it.

A cultural critic is usually someone who has been educated in the humanities and has focused his education and work life on some facet of the humanities. An art critic would have concentrated his work on art while a literary critic would have concentrated his work on literature. The critic will usually write or speak about the aspect of culture that he has studied while referencing biographical, historical, technical, and artistic standards by which he describes and analyzes the cultural work. Often the cultural critic will make positive or negative judgments about the cultural work, but usually the critic will, in his remarks, place the cultural work (and thus the efforts of that creator) into the context of the work's effects on human understanding as the critic sees it.

Essentially, the cultural critic is communicating how the cultural work has advanced (or not) the human enterprise. The student's examination of cultural criticism is sometimes an intimidating affair, as the student will encounter the writings and ideas of the critic who has spent a lifetime of work commenting on cultural artifacts, works, or especially the ideas of a particular creator of the culture being criticized. But the student should persevere and read or listen to the comments made, for often these comments will deepen the student's understanding of the research topic.

The student should be reminded that the cultural critic's opinion is just one perspective of the cultural work. The student can get a bigger picture of the cultural work when he considers more than one cultural critic's ideas. The student should be informed that cultural critics work in all areas of the creative human enterprise: art, literature, architecture, food, dance, music, technological innovations, communication, history, education . . . and the list could extend throughout the cultural universe. By learning what the cultural critic says about the creative work, and interacting, if possible, with the creative work itself, the student lays the intellectual groundwork for creating his own new ideas and understanding of the subject of his research.

## Workshop 6: What Is Culture and What Is Cultural Criticism?

**Learning Goals:** The goal of this workshop is the introduction of the concepts of culture and
  cultural criticism in the humanities.
**Location:** Classroom with whiteboard and projector
**Team:** Teacher, librarian, and library aide/resource guide
**Inquiry Unit:** As the selection of topic is made, students are introduced to basic humanities
  scholarly resources, especially cultural criticism.
**Total Time:** 50 minutes

| | |
|---|---|
| **Starter**<br>Time: 10 minutes<br><br>Inquiry<br>Community | The teacher begins the workshop by placing on a desk an original painting, a book, a large artisanal bread loaf, an elaborate garment, and so on. All represent culture. Then ask students, what is culture? What does culture mean to them and can they name some objects or work from their own culture? Perhaps the students could have a piece of the bread as food for thought.<br><br>The librarian will distribute **Handout #1: Tips for Encountering Cultural Criticism** and **Handout #2: List of Cultural Criticism Resources (Sample)** to be read aloud by the class. |
| **Work Time**<br>Time: 30 minutes<br><br>Inquiry<br>Community | During the work time, the librarian introduces the concepts of culture and cultural criticism with print or digital examples of cultural critics. This example might be of a work the student is already familiar with, having studied the work in a ninth- or tenth-grade class. Students (with the help of the librarian and the resource guide) can begin to examine critical work or reviews of their chosen topics. |
| **Reflection**<br>Time: 10 minutes<br><br>Inquiry<br>Community | Students gather together with the teacher and librarian to discuss how critics treated a particular work or creator of the work and whether the critic was being "fair." Why did the critic say what he said? Accessing, assimilating, and assessing information by cultural critics is often a major portion of humanities research. |
| **Notes:** | This work time is just the beginning. Another nonstructured workshop could be scheduled to permit students the time and guidance necessary to access, read, and analyze cultural criticism of the student's chosen topic. |

| Common Core Standards: | CCSS.ELA-LITERACY.RH.9-10.1<br>Cite specific textual evidence to support analysis of primary and secondary sources, attending to such features as the date and origin of the information.<br><br>CCSS.ELA-LITERACY.RH.9-10.6<br>Compare the point of view of two or more authors for how they treat the same or similar topics, including which details they include and emphasize in their respective accounts.<br><br>CCSS.ELA-LITERACY.RI.9-10.2<br>Determine a central idea of a text and analyze its development over the course of the text, including how it emerges and is shaped and refined by specific details; provide an objective summary of the text. |
|---|---|

# Workshop 6

## *Student Handout #1: Tips for Encountering Cultural Criticism*

You are about to begin serious research on some aspect of culture, how the cultural work(s) you have chosen and the cultural creator of that work influenced the United States of America. These tips may help you with your research:

1. Your topic is a cultural work or involves cultural work.
2. A cultural work is some object, work of art, speech, idea, political or social movement, activity, or organization of effort that reflects some aspect of culture.
3. A cultural creator is the individual(s) who thinks of and executes the cultural work.
4. Culture that is created is recognized as intellectual property.
5. As culture is created and then distributed for use by the public through publication, performance, etc., it becomes the object of judgment by cultural critics.
6. Cultural critics, for the most part, are trained to look at the cultural work and place the work in the context of the culture in which it is created to determine the influence of the work on the surrounding culture (and particularly the audience of the work).
7. Cultural critics may also review a cultural work to determine the influence of the surrounding culture on the cultural work itself.
8. Cultural critics may also compare the work to other works by the same creator or to other works by different cultural creators.
9. Because it is always beneficial to obtain more than one opinion, you should also read more than one cultural critic's ideas about a cultural work.
10. Cultural critics often work for daily newspapers, weekly or monthly magazines, and online blogs. You can find cultural criticism in the culture, style, or entertainment sections of these publications.

# Workshop 6

## *Student Handout #2: List of Cultural Criticism Resources (Sample)*

Cultural commentary and criticism can be found in multiple media such as newspapers, magazines, and radio and television programs. Education publication houses will create critical commentary series such as *Twentieth Century Literary Criticism.*

Newspapers: Large city newspapers both in print and online have sections of the paper that cover lifestyle stories and cultural news and events. Within these sections, cultural critics write reviews of recently published books; newly released music and technology; performances in dance, theater, and music; art shows and restaurant openings; and new examples of architecture, graphic design, and fashion. These reviews are considered cultural criticism. Newspapers also contain stories about the cultural creators.

Magazines: Magazines, particularly popular monthly magazines or magazines that focus on cultural subjects both in print and online also publish columns and articles that review culture and provide cultural criticism. For example, *Rolling Stone* magazine is a reliable source for music information as well as other pertinent cultural issues and *Sports Illustrated* is a reliable source for sports information and the business of sports. In addition, letters to the editor, responding to a previous issue's cultural content, are often written by cultural authorities who have educational and vocational expertise and are identified at the end of the letter to the editor, by name and role.

Documentary Films: Documentary films are often created to comment upon and criticize some aspect of society. Examples of social impact documentary films are: Errol Morris's *Thin Blue Line* about a death row inmate and a wrongful conviction; David Guggenheim's *An Inconvenient Truth* about Al Gore's efforts to educate the public about global warming; and Cynthia Hill's *Private Violence* about domestic violence.

Television: Television shows such as those on Public Broadcasting Service (PBS) that focus on investigative programming can be considered as commentary and may be produced by cultural critics. Bill Moyers's programs are such an example. Look on the PBS website for an archive of programming.

Radio Broadcasts: Radio shows such as those produced on National Public Radio (NPR) often contain interviews and commentary by cultural critics and cultural creators. Such broadcast transcripts can sometimes be found in the e-Library database.

Books: Books published in a series such as the *Twentieth Century Literary Criticism* (TCLC) or *Modern Critical Views* provide multiple critical essays about the works of authors, novelists, and dramatists.

Other reference-type book series located in the library's reference section cover the visual arts, photography, music, architecture, and the creative output of other cultural workers.

Online databases also contain much of the above-mentioned resources. One particular database, *Bloom's Literature* on Infobase Learning, recently won an award for educational software.

Databases in which many of these cultural resources can be found include:

EBSCO HOST
Green File
Academic Search Premier
Literary Reference Center

Proquest
Historical New York Times
International Edition

# Workshop 7

## Overview: Research in the Ubiquitous Media Environment

The goal of this workshop is to introduce students and teachers to the function of social media in the research process. A secondary goal of this workshop is to familiarize students with interrogating a range of contemporary online social media sources that may be used. This workshop requires students to approach research from a new angle. Students will not only use social media to search for information by using social media platforms as search engines, they will also engage with and interrogate information sources that have been published on social media websites and applications.

The world's media is now hyperconnected and socially shared. Globalization and advances in technology fuel the acceleration of hyperconnectivity. Information is created and spread across the globe instantaneously. While students are increasingly capable of producing meaningful media themselves, they often do not realize that they are constantly and superficially shifting awareness from one type of information source to another (Jenkins, 2006, 61). This inattention to the detail in information inhibits the students' ability to be wholly present as they constantly engage with new stimuli and encounter new information. Such is the consequence of information overload.

Dealing with information overload is a focus of media education to provide a basic understanding of information structure and the need for students to understand who creates and controls the flow of information, how information is stored and disseminated, and who has access to that information. Media education teaches the student how to evaluate information and determine whether or not it is reliable, because students need to understand that not everything they read is factual. This is especially true in social media. Students learn the essential social skill of understanding the vagaries of social media while engaging in responsible participation with media containing the cultural artifacts of society. Such responsible participation is a basic lesson in democracy and "civic engagement" (Jenkins, 2006, xii).

However, the teacher may find that students are more knowledgeable about trends in social media technologies and frequent those technologies more often than the teacher. This workshop is a collaboration between information guides (teacher and librarian) and information users (students), because the guide teaches the student how to evaluate and deconstruct messages contained in social media sources while the student teaches the guide about the platforms and emerging sources of social media.

For the purposes of this workshop, one event will serve as an example of how reporting a cultural event is manifest in social media. Three levels of reporting will be considered as primary, secondary, and tertiary sources. The example of the event is the 2014 People's Climate March in New York City, which will highlight various aspects of social media in the availability and variety of source types that researchers often seek.

The example of the 2014 People's Climate March also aims to highlight the variety of features of information disseminated in social media, the three types of information source(s), and the means for analysis of media content (Buckingham, 2003, 1) using a series of questions to interrogate online content transmitted through social media.

## Features of Information Dissemination

Students should be made aware that in their use of social media they will encounter three features of the media: *immediacy*, *objectivity*, and *interactivity* (Müller, 2014, 1). Information that is generated through social media, by an objective reporter, or on a blog will exemplify different characteristics. This is nuanced, as objective content generated by a journalist may also be published through social media, or a journalist might write and post content on his own blog. Students need to peel back each layer to understand various information structures.

In recognizing the three features of media, it is important for the student to remember that social media thrives on **immediacy**. In an instant, user-generated thoughts and feelings are broadcast around the world. Researchers have argued that constant connectivity is changing the way societies interact face-to-face. People seek instant gratification, personal connection, and informational updates, a desire social media fulfills, and that is why the Internet is overflowing with stream-of-consciousness information. The student must develop the skills necessary to determine what is useful and what is not. Meanwhile, a journalist's primary responsibility is to produce **objective** content. This type of information consists of carefully collected facts composed into narrative and reported by professionals. However, the integrity of journalistic endeavors has been questioned as media outlets that primarily depended on a tradition of objective edited journalism transition to online instantaneous publishing and 24/7 output. And finally, the blogosphere revolves around the **interactive** nature of user-generated comments. In virtual communities anyone can become a social critic and write a blog. Information is collected and shared in groups and with like-minded communities. User-generated comments are not necessarily credible but can be used to inform the researcher and further the researcher's hunt for information (Müller, 2014, 1).

**Students should also be made aware that larger media conglomerates now shape and control the flow of information worldwide. These conglomerates may manifest bias and may or may not depict diverse perspectives.**

## An Example of the 2014 People's Climate March

### Primary Source

**Source example:** *An activist from an advocacy group marches through the streets of Manhattan in the midst of the People's Climate March in September 2014 in New York City.*

This individual does not need to be a professional journalist and often will not be. The individual or group reports the event using various social sharing platforms that display text, audio, video, photographs, or a combination thereof. The person or group may have constructed a message with the intention of giving that message mass visibility so that it "goes viral" instead of simply providing information in and of itself for readers to use and further disseminate. A primary source (climate activist/advocate) gives the researcher a first-person perspective. The climate advocate(s) walks with other demonstrators, is immersed in the environment of the march (sees posters, artwork, performances, t-shirts, and buttons), and will disseminate information from his personal point of view.

**Dissemination of a Primary Source of Information:** The demonstrator/activist might use his phone to upload photos, audio, video, and short text posts to social networking websites or a virtual community that houses content that has been individually or collaboratively collected online. He may use a live stream to broadcast live video of the event. The demonstrator may also submit a blog post to a popular blogging website on location. Note that online postings might be uploaded in real time and indicate event location, or the location might be added once the event has ended.

Currently, social sharing platforms are accessible because most do not require paid subscriptions. The teacher "might want to discuss some background information regarding traditional (news) outlets and social media platforms and how the economic framing of these apparently 'free' services might influence the news generation and dissemination" (Müller, 2014, 1)

*In the workshop the student is encouraged to interrogate the primary, secondary, or tertiary sources so that the information provided can be analyzed. Each social media source should be evaluated to determine whether it is a primary, secondary, or tertiary source and only questions related to the source should be asked. For this Climate March example the following questions can apply.*

### Questions for a Primary Source:

1. Who is conveying the information (who is the primary source)?
2. What is the basic information conveyed in the source?
3. What message is the activist trying to convey?
4. Who is the activist speaking to with the media message?
5. What audience is the activist attempting to reach?
6. What social platforms does the activist use to reach people with his information?
7. Can you determine why this person or group is advocating for this specific cause?
8. What textual or nontextual cues do you pick up that help you determine this person or group's position, beliefs, or perspectives?
9. Can online users repost, edit, or use this content freely in any way? How can the information be reused?
10. What technology was used to create the content of this source?
11. Does the information appear to be accurate? How can you tell?

### Secondary Source

**Source example:** *A professional journalist who reports the Climate March from the sidelines.*

The journalist could be an employee of a media organization or a freelancer who sells individual pieces of work. This secondary source is responsible for objectively reporting an event. The journalist's opinion should not be reflected in the report but his perspective may be apparent. The journalist typically interviews two or more people to gain a sense of opposing viewpoints that will be included in the report.

**Dissemination of a Secondary Source of Information:** If the journalist collects information for a print edition story that will be published first on a website with social sharing capabilities, he will most likely wait to use the media organization's office resources to disseminate that story. Before the story is scheduled to appear in print, it may be posted on the media outlet's website prior to appearing in the morning edition of the newspaper. Note that the information published online may be subject to a different editorial process. Information published online, to keep up with the demand of twenty-four-hour news, may be less edited or edited for print after it has been published online. Alternatively, information that appears in print may become heavily editorialized. The researcher should be mindful of both these scenarios. Therefore, any source, whether online through social media or in print, should be balanced against other information sources to determine its accuracy.

### *Questions for a Secondary Source:*

**MEDIA OWNERSHIP**

1. What media outlet does the reporter work for?

2. Can you identify biases the news organization may have?

3. What audiences are reached through this outlet?

4. What audiences are left out?

**REPORTER**

1. Who is the reporter?

2. What is the basic information provided by the source?

3. What perspective does the reporter have?

4. Does the reporter assume a statement, scenario, or event is true or false?

5. Is the person being interviewed a primary or secondary source? (What is his authority?)

6. Is some information or another perspective missing from the report?

7. Can a diverse set of consumers relate to this information source or is it particular to a specific cultural value system or understanding?

## Tertiary Source

**Source example:** *A blogger who repurposes stories that already have been reported by primary and secondary sources.*

A tertiary source is the farthest perspective from the original event. While a tertiary source may rely on a mix of primary and secondary sources for information, he concentrates on secondary sources. Nonetheless, the tertiary source may provide a broader and/or deeper picture of the event aided by a larger, longer range perspective and other pertinent scholarship.

**Dissemination of a Tertiary Source of Information:** Dissemination of online tertiary sources can include mobile devices and computers.

It is important when utilizing a tertiary source to consider locating the original information source. Many blogs will repurpose nontextual work such as videos or photographs. In order to maintain accuracy, the student researcher should attempt to locate the original creator of that content and/or the original content, and analyze it from the first perspective. Finding information through tertiary sources is convenient and useful; however, it is important to trace the steps of the tertiary content creator.

*Questions for a Tertiary Source:*

Tertiary sources online vary in dissemination, reliability, and accuracy. The student researcher can use the same questions that would be used to interrogate a secondary source, as well as the following questions:

1. Who is the tertiary source? (What is his authority?)
2. Is the information dated?
3. Can you locate the original content?
4. Where does the author borrow information?
5. Does the author cite his borrowed information?
6. Has information from the original post been edited or omitted in the tertiary source?
7. If the source is nontextual (photographs, audio clips, or videos), is the information in its original form or has the information been altered?
8. How is the information framed or constructed? (The Center for Media Justice, 2014, 1)
9. Is the source part of a series of hyperlinks or part of a social network feed?
10. If the source appears in a social network feed, do the status and headline accurately represent the entire article?
11. Are there user-generated comments and are those comments relevant to your research?

The student can use these questions and other questions that are relevant to his topic and the media being analyzed and interrogated.

*Social media can be utilized by the student researcher in three ways: to disseminate information via social sharing platforms, to use as a search engine to locate information and satisfy informational needs, and to examine and use the information content itself. Typically students are more familiar with producing and sharing information than they are utilizing social media for research. Students are expected to understand both uses.*

**This workshop of ubiquitous social media is a lesson of analysis in the function of media producers and disseminators. This workshop requires students to slow down, observe, and interact with information that has already been shared and needs to be deconstructed and understood for its powerful nature.**

## Workshop 7: Research in the Ubiquitous Media Environment

**Learning Goals:** The goal of this workshop is to introduce students to the function of social media in the research process.
**Location:** Library or classroom
**Team:** Teacher, librarian, and resource guide
**Inquiry Unit:** This workshop aims to familiarize students with interrogating a range of contemporary online media sources that may be used in the research process.
**Total Time:** 50 minutes

| | |
|---|---|
| **Starter**<br>Time: 15 minutes<br><br>Inquiry<br>Community | The librarian shows the students a photograph, live-stream video, and audio clip from the People's Climate March, then asks the students what they know about the event. The librarian can ask students why they think the march occurred. Students can be shown environmentalist and social activist Bill McKibben's organizational website www.350.org to view some of the issues that instigated the march.<br><br>The librarian can gauge student media use by quickly asking students to call out what social sharing websites and applications they most frequently use, and what type of media they prefer to share (e.g., photos, videos, or audio).<br><br>Librarian should pass out 4x6 notecards. **Handout #1: Interrogation of Social Media Content** and **Handout #2: Glossary of Terms in Social Media** should be distributed. |
| **Work Time**<br>Time: 25 minutes<br><br>Individual<br>Scholars | Employing a search engine, students should locate (with assistance) a primary source and a secondary or tertiary source that is relevant to their chosen topic. The source should be one that has been disseminated through social media. Students should utilize hashtags, tags, and search boxes to locate material contained within a website or social media platform. A list of three sources and social media used should be marked on the note card. |
| **Reflection**<br>Time: 10 minutes<br><br>Inquiry<br>Community | The librarian can lead a discussion with students to determine what sources were found. Students should describe the steps they took to locate the sources. Students can discuss how this method of searching for information is different from other retrieval methods. Finally, the librarian can ask students, "What was helpful and what was difficult about using social media platforms to search for information with the interrogation sheet?" |

| Notes: | Until this point, most students of high school age use social media primarily to connect with friends and keep track of pop cultural figures, trends, and entertainment. The teacher, librarian, and resource guide should make students aware that the nature of this lesson has **nothing** to do with popular culture and everything to do with serious scholarly research. This is the first time most students are learning that social media can be used for research but this mental shift requires a different behavioral pattern with regards to how students use social media. Another unstructured workshop time can be scheduled to interrogate a social media website for their research topic information.<br><br>The teacher may choose another event to highlight in the workshop should environmental issues not be the teacher's choice. |
|---|---|
| **Common Core Standards:** | CCSS.ELA-LITERACY.WHST.9-10.8<br>Gather relevant information from multiple authoritative print and digital sources, using advanced searches effectively; assess the usefulness of each source in answering the research question; integrate information into the text selectively to maintain the flow of ideas, avoiding plagiarism and following a standard format for citation.<br><br>CCSS.ELA-LITERACY.SL.9-10.2<br>Integrate multiple sources of information presented in diverse media or formats (e.g., visually, quantitatively, orally), evaluating the credibility and accuracy of each source.<br><br>CCSS.ELA-LITERACY.L.9-10.6<br>Acquire and use accurately general academic and domain-specific words and phrases, sufficient for reading, writing, speaking, and listening at the college and career readiness level; demonstrate independence in gathering vocabulary knowledge when considering a word or phrase important to comprehension or expression. |

# Workshop 7

## *Student Handout #1: Interrogation of Social Media Content*

If you engage with social media you probably already know it is a powerful force that penetrates almost all aspects of daily life. It is important for students to learn how media is produced and spread across the globe. This awareness will help protect you from information overload while giving you the ability to decode the messages in the media you interact with.

Before information becomes an information source it exists as an observable event. Once a person interacts with an event and begins to formulate his own perspective or viewpoint about that event, an information source is created. An information source can be passed around the Internet by a professional or by a lay person in a variety of ways. People and organizations may hold a certain perspective or bias; thus it is important to remember that **all information is filtered and constructed by human experience**.

Social media deals with the construction of messages held in a variety of formats. Use these questions to interrogate social media sources and think about how media messages are created and disseminated to the public, as well as what content is delivered.

### Questions for a Primary Source

1. Who is conveying the information (who is the primary source)?
2. What is the basic information conveyed in the source?
3. What message is the activist trying to convey?
4. Who is the activist speaking to with the media message?
5. What audience is the activist attempting to reach?
6. What social platforms does the activist use to reach people with his information?
7. Can you determine why this person or group is advocating for this specific cause?
8. What textual or nontextual cues do you pick up that help you determine this person or group's position, beliefs, or perspectives?
9. Can online users repost, edit, or use this content freely in any way? How can the information be reused?
10. What technology was used to create the content of this source?
11. Does the information appear to be accurate? How can you determine this?

### Questions for a Secondary Source

#### Media Ownership

1. What media outlet does the reporter work for?
2. Can you identify biases the news organization may have?
3. What audiences are reached through this outlet?
4. What audiences are left out?

**Reporter**

1. Who is the reporter?
2. What is the basic information provided by the source?
3. What perspective does the reporter have?
4. Does the reporter assume that a statement, scenario, or event is true or false?
5. Is the person being interviewed a primary or secondary source? (What is his authority?)
6. Is some information or another perspective missing from the report?
7. Can a diverse set of consumers relate to this information source or is it particular to a specific cultural value system or understanding?

## Questions for a Tertiary Source

1. Who is the tertiary source? (What is his authority?)
2. Is the information dated?
3. Can you locate the original content?
4. Where does the author borrow information?
5. Does the author cite his borrowed information?
6. Has information from the original post been edited or omitted in the tertiary source?
7. If the source is nontextual (photographs, audio clips, or videos), is the information in its original form, or has the information been altered?
8. How is the information framed or constructed? (The Center for Media Justice, 2014)
9. Is the source part of a series of hyperlinks or part of a social network feed?
10. If the source appears in a social network feed, do the status and headline accurately represent the entire article?
11. Are there user-generated comments and are those comments relevant to your research?

# Workshop 7

## *Student Handout #2: Glossary of Terms in Social Media*

**Authority** – Authority refers to the credentials of experience, expertise, or education of the creator of the work or content.

**Comment** – A post that provides a response to a message contained within a social sharing platform.

**Construction** – The understanding that the process of creating media is man-made and is subject to individual perspectives and filters.

**Content creator** – Someone who makes some type of media (i.e. audio, video, photographs, design, etc.)

**Mass media** – The apparatus that disseminates messages to a broad number of people.

**Media message** – The core meaning of information held in a media product.

**Media multitasking** – Shifting awareness from one task to another, typically involving multiple media platforms or devices (Jenkins, 2006).

**Media outlet** – An arm of a large media company or a nonaffiliated media organization.

**Media ownership** – Relates to large conglomerates that increasingly buy small media outlets and reduce the diversity of ownership and thus the diversity of perspectives and voices that are represented.

**Medium** – A vessel that communicates text, sound, image, and/or video.

**Objective journalism** – A style of reporting that does not reflect the opinions or views of the reporter or media outlet.

**Original post** – The primary source of information from which other media was created.

**Social media** – Online applications and websites that enable users to form a social network and share content between users.

**Social network** – A network of online users that have the ability to communicate and interact with other users and their content.

**Social sharing platform** – An online space designed to contain a connected network of users who trade information and interact with one another.

**Status** – An update of information on a social sharing platform.

## Workshop 8

## Overview: Searching for Humanities Sources

The goal of this workshop is to introduce the student researcher to an array of different sources, both textual and nontextual, for the purpose of finding and using the sources to formulate and pursue the research question. This workshop begins with an introduction to several different kinds of sources and ends with a sort of treasure hunt to find the sources of information for the student's topic. *Teachers and librarians should keep in mind as they are advising students of possible sources that different learning styles are exhibited by students. Knowing the learning styles does not limit the student's choice of source types. Rather, knowledge of learning styles might help the guides to pique the student's interest and enlist early involvement by the student while steering the student to a source or sources that (at least initially) will be complementary to the student's learning style.* An example of this might be a student who displays a kinesthetic learning style and is interested in tap dancing as a possible topic. Rather than reading a biography of a tap dancer, a compatible first source may be a video of Savion Glover performing a modern tap dance.

As students begin to express interest in different topics, educators may use those topics to point out and explain different sources and to compile a list of possible sources by differentiating the information held in one source from the information held in another kind of source. Without casting judgment, the teacher may use three or more very different sources as illustrations for possible research and allow the student to determine which types of sources he will use. Let us take, for example, the subject of school integration in the mid-twentieth century. One source would be the Supreme Court ruling on the case of *Brown v. The Board of Education*. Another source could be a painting by Norman Rockwell titled *Ruby Bridges*. A third source could be newspaper coverage including photos of protests of school integration in Mississippi, and a fourth choice could be a video of the song "People Get Ready" by the Impressions.

At this stage in the research process it is most important that the student researcher be able to find multiple sources of information that are varied and hold the student's interest. As such, students can be given lists of possible sources, or the librarian can point out print and digital sources of texts, photos, art, music, or audio, steering the student to sources particular to the topic chosen. See **Handout #1: Historical Resources for the Humanities**.

**Handout #1: Historical Resources for the Humanities** is a list of some sources frequently used in humanities research. This list is a partial guide and it is not comprehensive. Teachers should encourage students to consult with librarians who are, after all, information retrieval experts and can serve as research guides. Another resource for humanities sources can be found in this book in **Workshop 13: Interrogating the Sources.** That workshop contains a number of student handouts that will assist the student in examining a wide variety of sources for information. The handouts in **Workshop 13** are called **Interrogation Sheets**.

## Workshop 8: Searching for Humanities Sources

**Learning Goals:** The goal of this workshop is to introduce the student to an array of different sources.
**Location:** Library
**Team:** Teacher, librarian, and resource guide
**Inquiry Unit:** This unit is part of the Selection Stage when the student ascertains that enough sources can be found to research his topic.
**Total Time:** 50 minutes

| | |
|---|---|
| **Starter**<br>Time: 15 minutes<br><br>Inquiry<br>Community | The teacher begins the workshop with a sample research topic and a very simple research question. The librarian will go to the board and ask students where they might look for sources. The teacher reminds students that their topics are to be considered in terms of the broader issue of what or how the topic affects an understanding of culture in the United States in the 21st century. Answers from students should be written on the board. **Handout #1: Historical Resources for the Humanities** of **Workshop 8: Searching for Humanities Sources** should be given to students. The librarian should also refer again to **Handout #1: List of Resources for a Humanities Research Paper (Sample)** of **Workshop 3: Encouraging a Variety of Sources and Formats** and **Handout #2: List of Cultural Criticism Resources (Sample)** of **Workshop 6: What Is Culture and What Is Cultural Criticism? Browsing for Ideas**. The librarian reminds students to use all three handouts. These handouts can be used in searching for sources. |
| **Work Time**<br>Time: 25 minutes<br><br>Individual scholars working with research guides | Each student, using the three handouts, should look for more sources for his chosen topic. This structured workshop can be continued in the next scheduled class period to ensure that students have enough search time. Resources that are print, digital, or three-dimensional may be searched now. Resources that may result in phone, personal, or e-mail interviews should then be scheduled. Content experts who may be subject teachers should be contacted. |
| **Reflection**<br>Time: 10 minutes<br><br>Study Buddies | During the reflection time, study buddies confer on their success or failure regarding search tactics and suggest other possibilities to one another. |
| **Notes:** | Certainly, scheduling at least one other nonstructured workshop for students to seek sources would be helpful. During the nonstructured workshops the teacher, librarian, and resource guide should circulate and offer assistance. |
| **Common Core Standards:** | CCSS.ELA-LITERACY.WHST.9-10.8<br>Gather relevant information from multiple authoritative print and digital sources, using advanced searches effectively; assess the usefulness of each source in answering the research question; integrate information into the text selectively to maintain the flow of ideas, avoiding plagiarism and following a standard format for citation. |

# Workshop 8

## *Student Handout #1: Historical Resources for the Humanities*

### Internet Sources

History Matters: A site curated by American Social History Project / Center for Media and Learning at City University of New York Graduate Center and the Roy Rosenzweig Center for History and New Media at George Mason University. History Matters includes a collection of annotated history links as well as a searchable primary source database *Many Pasts*. http://historymatters.gmu.edu/

Library of Congress: Education Resources: This Library of Congress page narrows the broad scope of the Library's massive digital collection for educators and students. Included on this page are links to primary source sets on popular topics in United States history as well as a Search by Standards feature that allows users to search for resources by State Standards Grade Level and discipline. http://www.loc.gov/education/

National Archives and Records Administration: Docs Teach: The National Archives curated collection, *Docs Teach*, includes searchable primary sources, online activities that can help students to interpret and corroborate evidence, and Document Analysis Worksheets written to help students analyze specific document types such as photographs, sound recordings, and cartoons. http://docsteach.org/

The Metropolitan Museum of Art: The Met, one of the largest and finest collections of art in the world, through the *Search the Collections* page, offers high-resolution images of works of art, related information, and multimedia content, and the locations of objects in the galleries. Also included on the site is the Heilbrunn Timeline of Art History where students can access short informational texts written by curators on a range of topics. The timeline can be searched by geographic location, time period, subject, artist name, and more. The Met's page is ideal for world history and world humanities projects. http://www.metmuseum.org

Internet History Sourcebook Project: A curated collection of open source historical texts from Fordham University, the Sourcebook Project is divided into separate categories such as Ancient History, Modern History, African History, and People with History: Lesbian, Gay, and Trans History. http://www.fordham.edu/Halsall/index.asp

The Gilder Lehrman Institute of American History: The institute's site offers many primary and secondary sources on United States history. Of particular note, the History Now page and the Gilder Lehrman Collection are easily searchable collections on the site. The former is the home of Gilder Lehrman's online magazine and is useful for secondary sources on particular themes. The latter collection is an archive of primary sources on United States history. https://www.gilderlehrman.org

### Online Databases

Cambridge Histories Online: This database includes more than 250 online versions of the *Cambridge Histories* series. A useful database for early phases of research, searchable texts offer scholarly reference overviews.

JSTOR: A database of more than 2,000 journals from the social sciences and humanities. JSTOR offers full-length articles for students to access but requires a paid subscription.

Library of Congress: American Memory: Designed as a database offering curated collections such as *Advertising, Cities and Towns*, and *Religion*. http://memory.loc.gov/ammem/index.html

Edtech teacher: Best of History websites: Edtech has curated and annotated a substantial collection of sites, of special interest are the sections *Primary Source Collections and Activities* and *History Museums Online*. Edtech has created a one-stop online site for students and teachers. http://www.besthistorysites.net/index.php/research

*Women and Social Movements in the United States, 1600–2000:* An online database published by the Center for the Historical Study of Women and Gender at SUNY Binghamton and Alexander Street Press with a focus on U.S. women's history between 1600 and 2000. The collection is home to over 4,000 documents and all materials are accessible through a 30-day free trial.

*Women and Social Movements, International*: Published by Alexander Street Press and requiring a login, WSMI offers an international scope for documents on women's history. http://womhist.alexanderstreet.com/

Academic Search Primer: This database is designed for academic institutions and offers a multidisciplinary collection of journals. ASP is useful for later research, as the site can be a bit intimidating even for seasoned researchers.

## Museums and Special Libraries

It is safe to say that there are thousands of museums and special libraries in the world. Some are public collections with enormous inventories in large cities; others are small, privately owned collections of oddities or singular subjects. Information on most humanities subjects can be found in the museums and special libraries, many of which can be accessed online.

Compiled by Joseph Schmidt,
Senior Instructional Specialist for Social Studies,
Office of Curriculum, Instruction, and Professional Learning,
New York City Department of Education, 2014

# Workshop 9

## Overview: The Research Question

The goal of the workshop is the student's statement of a distinct albeit simple research question based upon his preliminary reading and the searching he has accomplished thus far to find sources and identify materials from which he might borrow information.

The teacher should reassure the student that even at this point, he does not have enough information gathered, read, and processed to fully and eruditely pronounce a completely thought-out research question, although he has come far enough in his Information Search Process to go beyond stating, "This is my research subject." Now he should be able to ask a simple question of that research subject, a question that he would like to find an answer or answers for. He must continue his research in greater depth as he gathers more relevant information.

The workshop should not be about finalizing a research question but about beginning to articulate the question by first quickly examining some of the sources already found. For now, the student must determine the scope of the initial sources. The students have this time to sit down and experience some of the sources, listening to audio, watching video, reading introductions to works by the author, viewing photographs, or reading a speech. The student is beginning to sift through the sources to find points of interest.

At this time, the student is not yet making full notes as the note-taking lesson will be in **Workshop #12: Taking Notes and Keeping Track of Information**. Instead, the student is pursuing his sources in a leisurely manner to see or hear what catches his attention and piques his curiosity. A small set of sticky notes and the research notebook for keeping track of sources or questions that arise might be helpful as the student continues the initial interaction with his sources.

The teacher should remind the student to look for material that is interesting or surprising, and/or material that raises questions in the student's mind. Such material will make further research more interesting as the student begins to interrogate his sources as well as lending depth and meaning to the initial research question. The teacher and librarian encourage the student to latch onto the interesting, surprising, unusual, or questionable material and follow the information trail, not just in one source but perhaps in several sources, especially to see if that trail answers a question(s) the student might begin to formulate.

Those of us who have taught introductory research skills have sometimes witnessed paralysis caused by "confusion, frustration, or doubt" (Kuhlthau, 2004, 82) at this point. Expectations should not be too high. The teacher is simply asking the student to state one question about the subject which will lead him on a journey of discovery. That journey may not end with the question being answered neatly. In fact, at this point the student knows too little to determine if or how the question will be answered. For most student researchers, their simple question will morph into a different, possibly more complex question as the research continues. Eventually, that altered question and its answers can become the basis of a developed thesis statement with supporting or denying evidence. This is the beauty of guided inquiry. A student starting with little or no knowledge can research his way into a thesis and its supporting evidence.

## Workshop 9: The Research Question

**Learning Goals:** The goal of this workshop is the student's statement of a simple research question that will provide the basis for going beyond his browsing, choice of topic, and preliminary searching to further identify research materials.

**Location:** Classroom/Library

**Team:** Teacher, librarian, and research assistant

**Inquiry Unit:** The workshop takes place at the beginning of the Exploration Stage when the student begins to think about some of his first sources and determines a possible scope of his research.

**Total Time:** 50 minutes

| | |
|---|---|
| **Starter**<br>Time: 10 minutes<br><br>Inquiry Community | The Inquiry Community comes together in a seminar style to discuss why researchers might ask questions and if there is any difference between the questions a scientific researcher might have and the questions a humanities researcher might have. Teachers can ask students for possible humanities research questions and why questions might be asked. Student responses can be put on the board.<br><br>Teachers should have sample (and simple) humanities questions to model for the students. **Handout #1: Asking a Simple Question** should be provided and reviewed. |
| **Work Time**<br>Time: 30 minutes<br><br>Individual scholars and study buddies | During the work time, students can look at the resources they have found and begin a list of *simple* questions each would like to answer about the chosen topic. After creating a list of 2 or 3 questions, the student should sit with his study buddy and discuss each buddy's list of questions, getting feedback and advice. |
| **Reflection**<br>Time: 10 minutes<br><br>Inquiry Community | Students should again gather as an Inquiry Community and volunteer possible research questions to be placed on the board alongside the student's chosen topic. |
| **Notes:** | This workshop straddles two stages of the Information Search Process, coming at the end of the Selection Stage and the beginning of the Exploration Stage. Information Search Process guides should remain alert to those students who because of confusion, frustration, or doubt may need an intervention to continue the process. |

| Common Core Standards: | CCSS.ELA-LITERACY.W.9-10.2.B<br>Develop the topic with well-chosen, relevant, and sufficient facts, extended definitions, concrete details, quotations, or other information and examples appropriate to the audience's knowledge of the topic.<br><br>CCSS.ELA-LITERACY.W.9-10.7<br>Conduct short as well as more sustained research projects to answer a question (including a self-generated question) or solve a problem; narrow or broaden the inquiry when appropriate; synthesize multiple sources on the subject, demonstrating understanding of the subject under investigation.<br><br>CCSS.ELA-LITERACY.SL.9-10.1<br>Initiate and participate effectively in a range of collaborative discussions (one-on-one, in groups, and teacher-led) with diverse partners on grades 9–10 topics, texts, and issues, building on others' ideas and expressing their own clearly and persuasively. |
|---|---|

# Workshop 9

## *Student Handout #1: Asking a Simple Question*

This is your time to decide upon the simple question that will help to guide your research on your chosen topic.

My topic is: _____

_____

Five things I have learned so far in my research:

1. _____
2. _____
3. _____
4. _____
5. _____

The most interesting thing I have learned is: _____

_____

The most surprising thing I have learned is: _____

_____

The most unusual thing I have learned is: _____

_____

Some questionable or controversial information I have encountered: _____

_____

What aspect of my topic is not yet understandable? _____

_____

Do I need to sit down with a librarian or teacher to discuss this? ____Yes ____No

Two questions I have about my topic are:

*Question 1* _____

_____

*Question 2* _____

_____

Which question should I pursue as I continue my research?

_____

_____

# Research in the Exploration Stage of the Information Search Process

Workshop 10: Responsibility to Academic Honesty and the Problem with Plagiarism
Workshop 11: MLA Style and Formatting Paper
Workshop 12: Taking Notes and Keeping Track of Information

Three structured workshops are given during the Exploration Stage as students begin to seriously handle and view sources and take notes. All three workshops focus on the responsibilities of borrowing information for use in research projects and the skills needed to record and set aside the information the student chooses to borrow. After structured Workshop 12, two or more unstructured work times should be scheduled for students to actively take notes as they handle traditional textual sources and begin to interact with nontextual sources as well.

During the Exploration Stage the serious nature of students' responsibility to borrowed information should be underscored. By this we mean that students learn of the social, moral, and legal problems involved when borrowed information is not cited and listed on a works cited page and that the individual student is held accountable for all his information. Students will exhibit some confusion and frustration as they begin handling sources.

## Workshop 10

### Overview: Responsibility to Academic Honesty and the Problem with Plagiarism

*I have never thought about the responsibilities of explaining where you borrowed your information. I have only worried about plagiarism. Isn't that the scariest thing? The kids all think that plagiarism is the scariest thing. From the time they are in third grade they are afraid of it. Why? Plagiarism is like the boogeyman. Don't they know it's ok to use other people's stuff? Just make sure you thank them.*

Abbe Du Brow Branch, mother of former high school
students who are now college graduates

The goal of this workshop is the student's understanding of why the researcher is responsible to report the information he has borrowed, to "thank" the person from whom he is borrowing material. A secondary goal is to explain what plagiarism has to do with research and how to avoid getting into trouble.

At some early point in the academic life of any student, should that life include research and writing, a gigantic wrong must be righted. Somewhere in school, students and teachers must agree upon the unique idea behind research. That idea is the ability to borrow already existing information, to use that borrowed information to obtain newer ideas, to dwell in the joy of discovery of that which you borrowed and how it helps you to think about the world in a new way. When doing research the student must report what has been borrowed, where it was found, and what thoughts and ideas it produces. Research should be exciting and invigorating. Reporting on research should not be punitive or intimidating. Plagiarism and the fear it raises are not the key motivation for responsible research, although plagiarism is still fraud: it is hiding what has been borrowed. However, reporting what has been borrowed allows others to retrace the student's journey of discovery. This allows others to see the intellectual shoulders upon which the student stands, as his knowledge is built upon the foundation of someone else's previous knowledge.

A classroom narrative explaining the student's responsibilities to information and the problem of plagiarism can be voiced in the following manner:

A researcher reports what he has borrowed to thank his sources, to acknowledge that he is using the intellectual property of someone else, and to be accountable for how he uses that property. He is using and passing on the workings of someone else's mind.

The teacher may give the students a brief and simple, albeit necessary, explanation about plagiarism and intellectual property. This explanation is included in the following two paragraphs:

The problem with plagiarism is simple: plagiarism is theft. When you steal words, ideas, organization, sound, image, or any other intellectual output from someone else then you can get in trouble with the school. Each school has its own rules about stealing information but understand this: you must not borrow someone else's intellectual property by putting it into your own words, or your own video, or your own report without acknowledging it with a citation and a works cited listing. If you do not acknowledge what you borrowed, then you are claiming the information as your own. You are saying that the intellectual property came out of your own head. That is not right. You become a thief.

You are unlikely to get in trouble for too many citations, so anything you borrow, you cite. In a humanities research project, you will likely cite using the Modern Language Association's (MLA) handbook in print or online. **Workshop 11: MLA Style and Formatting Paper** will discuss MLA style and how your paper will look with your citations. In that workshop, students will practice MLA citations and learn how to cite what must be cited.

By using citations and making a works cited list, the researcher then leaves a trail of his sources and borrowed ideas just like the trail of cookie crumbs Hansel and Gretel left. Following the trail of ideas and sources, each researcher stands on the shoulders of previous researchers, and every new idea that is produced can proudly display the legacy of information that contributed to the new idea. Western civilization has depended upon this method of knowledge development for ages!

Early on, students should be exposed to the history of ideas and the responsibility of all scholars toward the borrowed information they use. Perhaps then the awful ogre of plagiarism can be diminished and students will fear research less as they understand the repercussions of plagiarism more.

## Workshop 10: Responsibility to Academic Honesty and the Problem with Plagiarism

**Learning Goals:** The goal of this workshop is the student's understanding of the academic responsibility to report in his paper the information he has borrowed and to consider, once again, the problem of plagiarism.

**Location:** Classroom

**Team:** Teacher, librarian, and possibly the dean or assistant principal

**Inquiry Unit:** This is the initial unit in the exploration stage as the student begins to delve into information sources.

**Total Time:** 35 minutes

| | |
|---|---|
| **Starter**<br>Time: 10 minutes<br><br>Inquiry<br>Community | The teacher and librarian will bring a printed copy or display a digital version of a recent article about academic dishonesty and the problem of plagiarizing in a research paper. Students will volunteer to read the article aloud.<br><br>The MLA handbook should be available and the MLA URL should be written on the board. All students should have source material with them. |
| **Work Time**<br>Time: 10 minutes<br><br>Inquiry<br>Community | The assistant principal or academic dean will briefly discuss the school's response to a plagiarism complaint and answer student questions about his statements. |
| **Reflection**<br>Time: 15 minutes<br><br>Inquiry<br>Community | The class will reflect on how to avoid plagiarism and how to properly account for borrowed information. Procrastination and the need for organization and time management should be referenced during the reflection period. |
| **Notes:**<br><br>Fifteen minutes remain in the regular period. | Students should present their sources. If time permits, students should read the pages in the MLA guide the teacher indicates. The teacher should refer to **Handout #1: Plagiarism Checklist** and inform students to use the handout as they write the research notes and paper. The teacher and librarian should circulate in the room to check the sources. Students may raise any questions about academic honesty for the teacher and librarian to answer. The next lesson will be a discussion of the MLA Style for writing a research paper. |

| Common Core Standards: | <u>CCSS.ELA-LITERACY.W.9-10.8</u><br>Gather relevant information from multiple authoritative print and digital sources, using advanced searches effectively; assess the usefulness of each source in answering the research question; integrate information into the text selectively to maintain the flow of ideas, avoiding plagiarism and following a standard format for citation.<br><br><u>CCSS.ELA-LITERACY.SL.9-10.3</u><br>Evaluate a speaker's point of view, reasoning, and use of evidence and rhetoric, identifying any fallacious reasoning or exaggerated or distorted evidence. |
| --- | --- |

## Workshop 10

### *Student Handout #1: Plagiarism Checklist*

Borrowing information is at the heart of developing new knowledge. As long as you credit an author's information and concepts, and do not claim them as your own, you should not feel apprehensive about borrowing people's ideas! It is important for every researcher to learn how to properly credit borrowed information. Below is a checklist to help you determine if you are taking the right steps to credit your borrowed information. **Use this list as you begin writing your notes and your paper.**

1. Did you cite *all* borrowed material that is not your own? This includes definitions and concepts that you were not already aware of. You will need to include citations for:

    ___ All text that is directly quoted

    ___ All text that is paraphrased (put into your own words)

    ___ All text that includes phrases or terms that are not common knowledge to your reader

    ___ Any organization or graphics that you used

    ___ Any images or sounds that you used

2. ___ Did you use the Modern Language Association (MLA) Style method of citation for humanities research?

3. ___ If you did not, did you use another citation style for humanities research recommended by the teacher?

4. ___ Did you use parenthetical in-text citations after borrowed information? In-text citations will vary depending on the author, number of authors, type of work. See an MLA Style handbook for specific citation instructions.

5. ___ Did you start a reference list or works cited page, with complete bibliographic information, to keep track of all borrowed sources so that your reader can retrace your research and you are held accountable for it?

While some teachers may closely examine your paper for plagiarism, others will use computer-generated programs. These programs scan the document for borrowed information. **When in doubt, always cite material.** The citation can always be removed by a teacher or librarian after the first draft is handed in. No person has yet failed a paper for overciting.

# Workshop 11

## Overview: MLA Style and Formatting Paper

The goal of this workshop is to introduce students to a style manual. For some students, this is the first time they may physically handle a Modern Language Association style manual. In scholarly research, it is imperative that sources are adequately documented in the body of the scholarly papers, as well as on a works cited page(s) at the conclusion of the paper. It is equally important to follow a set of style standards to carefully present the information in the paper. There are several style guides used in different areas of research such as the Modern Language Association (MLA) manual, the American Psychological Association (APA) manual, and the Chicago Manual of Style.

The style manual of the Modern Language Association is a premiere humanities style manual. Because it is a guide, it is written as a self-help work and describes how to prepare and present a humanities research paper. The standards and rules that are found in the MLA style manual include the answers to these questions:

1. Is the cover page in good shape with all the information? (Title of the paper, student's name, the teacher's name, course title, and date the paper is handed in).

2. Is the header (which is the last name of the paper's author and the page number) set on the top of each page?

3. Are the pages set up in a uniform way with correct spacing, margins, and indentation?

4. Is the font uniform and the appropriate size?

5. Is each section of the paper indicated with a heading?

6. Are the in-text citations properly formatted?

7. Do the citations of the sources fully appear on the works cited page as well?

8. Are the sources correctly formatted and fully listed on the works cited page?

You, as the teacher, may point out other standards of style you may wish to include in the paper. The MLA guide will assist you with this. Both the teacher and student may access the MLA style manual in print or online. The above questions constitute the student **Handout 1: Style Questions the MLA Manual Will Help to Answer**.

## Workshop 11: MLA Style and Formatting Paper

**Learning Goals:** The goal of this workshop is to introduce the student to a style manual and the MLA standards of a research paper.

**Location:** Library

**Team:** Librarian and teacher

**Inquiry Unit:** In this workshop during the Exploration Stage, as the student first handles materials to be used in the research paper, he learns he must cite in the MLA style. The MLA manual is a necessary resource and, therefore, is introduced here.

**Total Time:** 50 minutes

| | |
|---|---|
| **Starter**<br>Time: 20 minutes<br><br>Inquiry Community | The librarian begins the workshop by setting in front of the students several copies of different style manuals such as the MLA, APA, and Chicago Manual of Style. The librarian explains how different fields of knowledge and disciplines of knowledge use different rules to report their research and to write about the knowledge discovered. He explains that the MLA style manual will be used for the current research project. He passes around the MLA style manual, **Handout #1: Style Questions the MLA Manual Will Help to Answer** and **Handout #2: Sample of Works Cited Entries for Your Reference List.** Students are informed that the material is a self-help guide and a go-to text, either in print or online, to answer style questions, citation problems, and how the paper should be formatted. |
| **Work Time**<br>Time: 15 minutes<br><br>Study Buddies | During the work time each study buddy pair should write an in-text citation and a works cited listing for at least one source that the study buddy is using and be prepared to write that information on the board. |
| **Reflection**<br>Time: 15 minutes<br><br>Inquiry Community | During reflection, each student will enter one borrowed information sentence with a citation on the board to be critiqued. Students may then reflect on the ease of citations and that the "ogre of plagiarism" can now be banished. |
| **Notes:** | The workshop is only the beginning of the student self-guiding his responses to borrowed information and his paper into MLA style. Individual students may need further help or tutorials with the teacher or librarian. Time should be scheduled for such help. |

| Common Core Standards: | CCSS.ELA-LITERACY.WHST.9-10.8<br>Gather relevant information from multiple authoritative print and digital sources, using advanced searches effectively; assess the usefulness of each source in answering the research question; integrate information into the text selectively to maintain the flow of ideas, avoiding plagiarism and following a standard format for citation.<br><br>CCSS.ELA-LITERACY.W.9-10.1.D<br>Establish and maintain a formal style and objective tone while attending to the norms and conventions of the discipline in which they are writing. |
| --- | --- |

# Workshop 11

## *Student Handout #1: Style Questions the MLA Manual Will Help to Answer*

The Modern Language Association style manual is a premiere humanities style manual. The manual is written as a self-help guide. It describes how you write a humanities paper. The standards and rules that are found in the MLA style manual include the answers to these questions:

1. Is the cover page in good shape with all the information? (Title and name, teacher, class, and date)
2. Is the header (which is the last name of the paper's author and the page number) set?
3. Are the pages set up in a uniform way with correct spacing, margins, and indentation?
4. Is the font clear and the appropriate size?
5. Is each section of your paper indicated with a heading?
6. Are the in-text citations properly formatted?
7. Do the sources appear correctly formatted in a works cited page?

**You can consult a print version of the style guide or go to the MLA website.**

A key function of a style manual is showing the reader how and where to cite information as well as the look and organization of the works cited page. Most online citation generators will create citations in multiple styles. We have included a sample of the EasyBib works cited entries in MLA style in **Handout 2: Samples of Works Cited Entries for Your Reference List**.

# Workshop 11

## *Handout #2: Samples of Works Cited Entries for Your Reference List*

**EasyBib**    **MLA Examples** of Popular Sources

### TV/Radio

**MLA**    "Episode." Contributors. *Program.* Network. Call Letter, City, Date. Medium.

**Ex:**    "The Saudi Experience." Prod. Mary Walsh. *Sixty Minutes*. CBS. WCBS, New York, 5 May 2009. Television.

### Film

DVD, Film etc.

**MLA**    *Title.* Contributors. Distributor, Year of release. Medium viewed.

**Ex:**    *The Dark Knight.* Dir. Christopher Nolan. Perf. Christian Bale, Heath Ledger, and Aaron Eckhart. Warner Bros., 2008. DVD.

### Sound Recording

MP3, CD etc.

**MLA**    Contributors. "Song." *Album.* Band. Manufacturer, Year. Medium.

**Ex:**    Corgan, Billy, and Butch Vig. "Today." *Siamese Dream*. Smashing Pumpkins. Virgins Records America, 1993. CD.

### Visual Art / Photograph

**MLA**    Last, First M. *Painting.* Year created. Medium of work. Museum / collection, City.

**Ex:**    Picasso, Pablo. *Three Musicians*. 1921. Oil on panel. Museum of Mod. Art, New York.

### Lecture / Speech

**MLA**    Last, First M. "Speech." Meeting / Organization. Location. Date. Description.

**Ex:**    Obama, Barack H. "Inaugural Address." 2009 Presidential Inaugural. Capitol Building Washington. 20 Jan. 2009. Address.

**EasyBib**        **MLA Examples** of Popular Sources

## Interview

|                     | If any | Magazine, newspaper, television information |

**MLA**   Interviewee. "Title." Interview by interviewer. Publication information. Medium.

**Ex:**   Abdul, Paula. Interview by Cynthia McFadden. *Nightline*. ABC. WABC, New York. 23 Apr. 2009. Television.

## Cartoon

|                     | If any | Magazine, newspaper, book |

**MLA**   Last, First M. "Title." Cartoon / Comic strip. Publication information. Medium.

**Ex:**   Trudeau, Garry. "Doonesbury." Comic strip. *New York Times* 8 May 2008: 12. Print.

*Note that all months in MLA are abbreviated except for May, June and July. For example, "February" is "Feb."

Cite your sources at *www.easybib.com*

# Workshop 12

## Overview: Taking Notes and Keeping Track of Information

The goal of this workshop is the student's understanding of how to take notes for humanities research. The student learns to keep track of and fully utilize the information he wishes to borrow from his research. Note-taking is an essential skill for the student to practice because it is a skill that he will use throughout his academic and working life.

Generally, notes are taken to keep track of and remember items, descriptions or details, or facts for future use. Because these notes contain borrowed information that originated with someone else, the note must contain not only the message of the information but also the source or originator (author, artist, or creator) of the information as well as indicate the package the information is held in and where the note's information was found. Because a note is not usually big or long, all this information should be positioned in some way that is in one spot for the researcher and easily recognizable. He will eventually organize and place in preferred order the notes to present his research and to harvest from that research some of his own ideas about the research topic, his research question, a thesis, and eventually, provide support or denial of the research thesis.

Note-taking may be considered the biggest task of the humanities research project, a task that is repeated over and over as the project comes together. It is a task that is essential for the successful completion of a research project. But many students hate, absolutely hate, taking notes and view it as an unnecessary and time-consuming make-work task. It falls on the teacher and librarian to explain the centrality of note-taking for the completion of the research project. Some actual note-taking lessons may remind students that the task is not so onerous, when combined with time-saving tips to make the task easier.

In an effort to make this workshop as easy as possible and for the student to be able to keep track of what is on the notecards or other forms of notes, the lesson begins.

## Workshop 12: Taking Notes and Keeping Track of Information

**Learning Goals:** In this workshop the student is introduced to three types of note-taking for use of borrowed information: 1) quote, 2) paraphrase, and 3) summary note.

**Location:** Library

**Team:** Teacher, librarian, and resource guide

**Inquiry Unit:** In this workshop the student learns to make notes from borrowed information, so that he can use this skill in transferring received information into his own written notes.

**Total Time:** 50 minutes

| | |
|---|---|
| **Starter** <br> Time: 10 minutes <br><br> Inquiry Community | The librarian and teacher bring in one favorite short quote each and write it on the board. After the quotes are on the board, student volunteers are called upon to paraphrase each quote. Five 4x6 notecards are handed out to each student. <br><br> The librarian distributes **Handout #1: Six Tips for Humanities Research Note-Taking, Handout #2: Research Note-Taking Activities (Part I)**, and **Handout #3: Research Note-Taking Activities (Part II)**. |
| **Work Time** <br> Time: 25 minutes <br><br> Study Buddy and Inquiry Community | Students are broken up into study buddy pairs. Using the notecards, each study buddy first gives a two-sentence quote that is from his own imaginary book. Using the teacher's model, the student will then place the author's name (the study buddy's name) on the upper left-hand corner. The student will put the name of the study buddy's made-up book and the page number of the quote on the bottom right-hand corner. The card is complete. The students switch roles. After each has created a direct quote note, each must use that quote note to paraphrase the quote (put the quote into his own words.) <br><br> Examples of student-generated direct quote notes and subsequent paraphrase notes will then go on the board. Inquiry Community discusses how difficult it is to paraphrase and how important it is not to cheat by plagiarizing. The whole community is asked to make a summary note of 2–3 sentences about what happened in the workshop session. <br><br> Students should be informed that this workshop marks the beginning of taking research notes of all borrowed material. They should be told that they are expected to create a minimum of *at least* 100 notes and as many as 200 notes during the course of their research project. Only 20% of them should be quote notes. They will probably make more notecards than they use because weaker or less important notes will be edited (weeded) out. Students will have three weeks to make research (borrowed information) notes. One helpful way to keep track of sources used for the notecards is by color coding the sources, either using a different color notecard for each different source or by using different color highlighters on the card or notebook to indicate each different source. |

| | |
|---|---|
| **Reflection** <br> Time: 15 min <br><br> Inquiry <br> Community | Students reflect as a community on the act of note-taking. |
| **Notes** | Each notecard should contain only *one* idea of 1–4 sentences in length. This is very important for the subsequent "Organizing Notes" lesson. |
| **Common Core Standards:** | CCSS.ELA-LITERACY.SL.9-10.1 <br> Initiate and participate effectively in a range of collaborative discussions (one-on-one, in groups, and teacher-led) with diverse partners on grades 9–10 topics, texts, and issues, building on others' ideas and expressing their own clearly and persuasively. <br><br> CCSS.ELA-LITERACY.W.9-10.8 <br> Gather relevant information from multiple authoritative print and digital sources, using advanced searches effectively; assess the usefulness of each source in answering the research question; integrate information into the text selectively to maintain the flow of ideas, avoiding plagiarism and following a standard format for citation. |

# Workshop 12

## *Student Handout #1: Six Tips for Humanities Research Note-Taking*

While the task of taking notes may not be the favorite task of the student researcher, nonetheless some note-taking tips make the job easier or at least more understandable. Six tips should be considered and discussed in class prior to the start of collecting borrowed information by taking notes. The individual teacher may have other tips to add or may alter these six tips.

Tip 1: Regardless of whether notes are prepared on notecards and handwritten, on a computer and placed in a notebook, or digitally prepared with a program such as Evernote, each note should contain information about ***only one idea.***

Tip 2: Each note should be only one to three or four sentences long, if possible.

Tip 3: All notes should be written as full sentences. If bullet points are necessary, they should be incorporated into sentence structure.

Tip 4: Only 10–20% of your notes should be quotations. The rest of the notes should be in your own words, either as paraphrased short passages or paraphrased longer summaries.

Tip 5: Your notes on borrowed information should contain information, etc. that is interesting to you and informative to your reader—**not stuff you already know**. After all, these are **researched** notes.

Tip 6: You are creating many of your notes from cultural critical sources. This paper is neither a biography nor a simple narrative. It is about what cultural sources and cultural criticism have said about your topic.

# Workshop 12

## *Student Handout #2: Research Note-Taking Activities (Part I)*

### Direct Quote Note Activity:

Pair up with your study buddy. Without showing each other, make up an imaginary book written by your study buddy. On the notecard, write the author's (buddy's) last name, the title of the book, and the page number, as well as a direct quote from his/her book (with quotation marks). You "make up" your study buddy's quote. Then take turns sharing your direct quotes with the rest of the class, making sure to include all of the necessary information. On the back of this card and all future notecards you make, you may write the question that this quotation, paraphrase, or summary note answers. **No more than 20% of your notes should be direct quotes.**

### Paraphrase Note Activity:

The term "paraphrase" is explained.

Again, work with your study buddy. In this activity, you invent another title of your own book and invent a quote or use the previously invented quote. Your buddy writes down your quote and bibliographic information on a notecard. Then, your buddy must paraphrase the quote that you created on a second notecard. Switch roles and repeat the process. The cards are shared aloud with the class. It is important to stress that when you paraphrase, you cannot use any of the same words unless the words are proper nouns that are in the direct quote. Also, **notes on cards must be in complete sentences.**

**Summary Note Activity:**

The term "summary" is explained.

You must now summarize the entire lesson in a few sentences. You must be sure to include all pertinent bibliographical information.

Example:

---

Author's Last Name                              **(Absolutely Leave Space Blank)**

Notecard Format

- The note itself goes here.
- Record **one idea** per notecard.
- "Quotes" if quoted, must have quotation marks around the info.
- Ten percent of all the notecards may be quote notes.
- Full sentences must be used in note cards.
- Avoid bullet points if possible on your note cards.

*Source Title or Source #
Page # of Information!

---

Remember: Notes can be made from texts, interviews, observations, programs, class lectures, pictures, movies, music, and conversations. **You are still borrowing material in all of these circumstances.**

In total, 100–200 notecards should be made, possibly more than you need. You may color-code or letter-code your sources or the notecards to keep yourself organized. You will probably not use all of your notes for your paper because you will edit out the unnecessary information before writing your paper.

# Workshop 12

## *Student Handout #3: Research Note-Taking Activities (Part II)*

1. Direct quote note: Copy the *exact words* from sentences you wish to use. Put quotation notes around them "like this." **Only quote one idea per notecard**. Can be 1–4 sentences.

2. Paraphrased note: Rewrite sentence(s) using your own words. Only use and paraphrase one idea per notecard. Use full sentences. Can be 1–3 sentences.

3. Summarized note: Take several sentences or paragraphs and summarize in your own words. Use full sentences. Can be 1–3 sentences.

## Research in the Formulation Stage of the Information Search Process

Workshop 13: Interrogating the Sources
Workshop 14: Further Developing the Research Question into a Thesis Using Ideas Uncovered
    While Interrogating the Sources

In the Formulation Stage of the Information Search Process, the student researcher is interacting with his sources to mine them for information he may use. With that information, he is able to better articulate a research question and create a thesis using the articulated research question and how the information he has found might answer it.

During formulation, clarity of what is being researched grows as do the focus and interest of the student. At this stage, teacher and librarian should be watching for individual students who are not displaying such behaviors. Individual tutorials should be set for students who need more help.

# Workshop 13

## Overview: Interrogating the Sources

The goal of this workshop is the student's introduction to the concept of interacting with each source, either textual or nontextual, by applying questions that are pertinent to the source and to the format in which the information is held. Because the information environment itself is so much richer and the information is so much more accessible to modern students, these two conditions do not imply that modern students know what to do with the data they receive or how to mine that data to get the most meaningful information from it. While a sixteen-year-old may know what type of car he wants and even know what he will choose to do with that car when he finds it, that does not mean he knows how to drive the car and navigate the car to his best advantage. Useful sources of information may be found and gathered with or without help from teachers and librarians. But once the sources are gathered, the student may be at a loss as to what kind of information he can get from the sources and how to handle the sources.

Twenty-first century information sources are ever expanding, and access to those sources is increasing exponentially. In both the humanities and sciences, scholars and teachers are producing more and more knowledge which, through a variety of means of packaging and distribution, becomes available to the public. This lesson focuses on how to obtain information from multiple sources by "interrogating" (questioning) each source in a manner of awareness of its nature and its capability of transmitting different types of information.

The lesson is essentially about formulating questions that, when addressed to the particular information source by the researcher, will produce in the researcher a first-person response based almost wholly upon the source being interrogated and the student's observational powers. Such a question/response approach to a source does not supplant traditional text-based research. Instead, it broadens the research and enhances or deepens the response to both textual and non-textual sources.

Examples of nontextual sources of information include garments, artifacts, performances, music, art, political graphics, photographs, sports events, and speeches. While other nontextual sources may be researched, these examples provide both teacher and student with a broad sense of possible nontextual sources of research. When any of these sources are researched, the student who first encounters the source may be practiced enough to handle the source and get the information from it that is needed. However, that is often not the case. A student will find a photograph, retrieve a garment, or enter a performance not having the faintest idea how to handle the source, what to look for, or what to gain from the source.

Additionally, for a researcher without deep knowledge of the topic being researched, the very idea of what the basic research question is may be vague or inarticulate. As the researcher encounters various sources of different types, that research question may begin to come into focus. Therefore, the librarian and teacher must prepare the student researcher to interact with his sources by first asking each source questions particular to that source. For example, the questions a student researcher will ask of a garment will be different from the questions that will be asked of a musical performance. Second, the librarian and teacher must encourage interpretation of the information without providing such an interpretation to the student researcher.

For example, say a student is researching United States Civil War uniforms. He visits a museum and sees a Union soldier's jacket. So, what now? How does he learn something from that jacket, other than the small identification of museum curation that is tacked to the case holding the jacket? What can the student note about the jacket to add to his paper? How can he interact with the jacket—or any other nontextual source—to build his knowledge about his research topic? And above all, what information can he borrow from the jacket to join with all of his other borrowed information and provide him with a fuller picture of his research topic?

During a criminal investigation, sources are questioned to gather information about a crime. The more precise the questions that are asked, the better the criminal investigation becomes as it moves toward solving the mystery of the crime. Detectives use interrogation methods to ask questions, gather more pertinent information, and formulate other, more precise questions whose answers lend themselves to solving the crime.

Researchers are a lot like detectives. The researcher investigates (or studies) some unknown topic. A researcher who has obtained a source of information must now interrogate that source, ask some general questions and after general information is received, ask some more precise questions to add to his body of knowledge about what he is researching. This interrogation (the questioning of his source) will provide the researcher with answers that help him solve the mystery, or at least part of the mystery, of what his research subject is all about.

Too often, teachers and librarians assume that students will know what to do with information sources, and therefore, fail to provide specific guidance to the student researcher. The student is left on his own. The interrogation sheets contained in this workshop will begin to provide the guidance needed. Each sheet addresses the interrogation of one particular type of source with questions directed to that information source. For example, say that a student is researching the photographer Diane Arbus. The student will find on **Interrogation Sheet #12: Interrogating a Photograph** specific questions to ask a single Diane Arbus photograph.

Sixteen interrogation sheets have been assembled for this workshop with questions formulated by teachers who regularly use and teach the types of information sources being interrogated. For example, **Interrogation Sheet #5: Interrogating a Garment** was created by an award-winning costume designer and high school drama teacher, and **Interrogation Sheet #3: Interrogating a Coin or Pottery Sherd** was written by a Latin teacher who has participated in archeological digs in Greece.

While multiple interrogation sheets are presented in this workshop, each student may use only one or two, depending upon the sources he has gathered. Each interrogation sheet begins with general, introductory questions that will establish the identity and authority of the source (i.e., what is it and who "made" it). More specific or precise questions follow on the interrogation sheet which the student must address to the source. Then—and here is the truly interactive aspect—the student, through his observational or experiential powers, must answer how he interacts with the source vis-à-vis the question he asks the source.

Notes should be taken and kept, at least one note for each question asked. The note begins with the question and is completed with the observational or experiential answer of the student researcher.

The questions on the interrogation sheets are suggested questions. As the interrogation of the source continues, other revised and/or original questions may arise in the student's mind. This is wonderful because it means that the student is now so engaged with his source that he is thinking on his own! His original questions may then lead to even more original responses to the source and to the student's generated interpretations of the sources, all of which should be noted for the research paper.

Among the interrogation sheets in the student handouts for this workshop are questions for both textual and nontextual sources. Teachers should feel free to create other sheets to interrogate other sources not included herein. Teachers should encourage students to add other questions through their own observational experiences and newfound informational base of knowledge.

For teachers and students, the interrogation of a nontextual source will often provide a gateway into other sources of information, both textual and nontextual. If, for example, a researcher interested in dance views video clips of a George Balanchine choreographed ballet, the student may subsequently read a critical review of the ballet or find a book of photographed ballet costumes and sets from Balanchine's ballets. Teachers and librarians can guide students from one interrogation of a nontextual source to another interrogation of a textual source. With this method, the information search process can maximize the potential for students to interact with multiple sources and formats of information in a meaningful way.

## Workshop 13: Interrogating the Sources

**Learning Goals:** The goal of this double workshop is the introduction to the concept of interrogating an information source and the student's initial efforts to interrogate a source.

**Location:** Library

**Team:** Teacher, librarian, and resource guide (in the first workshop period, the photography teacher)

**Inquiry Unit:** During this workshop, which constitutes the beginning of the Formulation Stage, students are focusing on useful materials as they gain clarity about the direction of their research. Their information search process begins to take on deeper purpose.

**Total Time:** 100 minutes (two workshop periods)

| | |
|---|---|
| **Starter**<br>Time: 35 minutes<br><br>Inquiry Community | The teacher and librarian spread copies of each of the sixteen interrogation sheets on a table. The teacher begins a discussion with the students about a crime and what occurs afterwards when detectives are investigating the crime. |
| **Work Time**<br>Time: 55 minutes<br><br>Inquiry Community | The librarian then opens a discussion of the difference between textual and nontextual sources of information and asks the students for examples of nontextual sources of information, placing their source responses on the board. Each student is then provided with a sheet of paper. The photography teacher will display a digital copy of a famous photograph of the placing of the American flag on the moon or some other iconic photograph. On a split screen the photography teacher or librarian will display **Interrogation Sheet #12: Interrogating a Photograph**. Using the photograph, students are asked to answer the questions on the interrogation sheet as the photography teacher walks students through the sheet, answering student questions and clarifying misunderstandings the students may experience.<br><br>During the next sixty minutes of workshop time (spread over two days) each student will choose a single interrogation sheet that he might use for his research. Working with the librarian and his study buddy, the student determines a source that would be applicable and, if possible, accesses the source to begin the interrogation. He confers with his study buddy who will assist the interrogation and who will ask for assistance while he is interrogating his own source. |
| **Reflection**<br>Time: 10 minutes<br><br>Inquiry Community | Teacher, librarian, and students gather with their interrogation sheets to share their experiences and ask questions if needed. |

| Notes: | Another one or two unstructured workshop times can be added to complete the notes or interrogations and possibly initiate other, new interrogations. |
| --- | --- |
| | Each researcher may use 1–5 different interrogation sheets. |
| **Common Core Standards:** | CCSS.ELA-LITERACY.W.9-10.8<br>Gather relevant information from multiple authoritative print and digital sources, using advanced searches effectively; assess the usefulness of each source in answering the research question; integrate information into the text selectively to maintain the flow of ideas, avoiding plagiarism and following a standard format for citation.<br><br>CCSS.ELA-LITERACY.RH.9-10.2<br>Determine the central ideas or information of a primary or secondary source; provide an accurate summary of how key events or ideas develop over the course of the text. |

# Workshop 13: List of Interrogation Sheets

1. Allusion
2. Work of Art
3. Coin or Pottery Sherd
4. Realistic Fiction
5. Garment
6. Graph
7. Interview
8. Legal Document
9. Live or Recorded Musical Performance
10.  Natural Phenomenon
11. Textual Source of Nonfiction
12. Photograph
13. Political Cartoon
14. Live or Recorded Speech, or a Transcript of a Speech
15. Live or Recorded Sporting Event
16. Live or Recorded Theater Performance

# Workshop 13

## *Student Handout #1: Interrogating an Allusion*

*An allusion demands investigation. An allusion does not produce meaning by itself.*

Derek Martin

Before we can interrogate an allusion, we must understand what an allusion is and its purpose(s) in the literature at hand. An allusion is a direct reference (though sometimes subtle) to something outside the story that lends context and, therefore, a deeper layer of meaning to the story. Often, however, that context can be surprising on many levels.

The "something outside the story" is often, but not always, a thing usually identified by a proper noun—as in an actual person, a geographical location, or other noted piece of literature or work of art. Obviously, the capitalization of any name or place is a clue to a proper noun and also an allusion, though again, allusions can be made in much more covert ways. The problem is, the word itself is either mysterious or seems misplaced, even random, and is often overlooked by the student as incidental or not important.

For example, let us examine Tennessee Williams's play *The Glass Menagerie*. When Tom (the protagonist and narrator) sets the scene, he speaks directly to the audience, declaring "In Spain there was Guernica." Because the play is set in St. Louis, Missouri, Tom's reference seems out of place. However, a close reader will dissect the sentences around this statement and detect that Tom is talking about revolution. The idea of revolution is being established early in the play, and eventually the action will depict Tom's own inward and outward personal revolutions.

To review, at this point Williams has given us a geographical reference to a place in Spain while establishing the location and action of the play in St. Louis. This does indeed seem random, or at least odd. The vast majority of student readers of *The Glass Menagerie* will forgo investigating exactly what Guernica is, and in fact many will never give it a second thought. Yet, this is exactly what should not happen. We must investigate and discover hidden meaning in the text.

So the first question is: what is Guernica? What is wonderful about researching an allusion is that students are only one click away from discovery. A simple search engine inquiry will enlighten us in many ways. The thing that pops up most often is Pablo Picasso's painting *Guernica*. Ok, so it's a painting. But is that all? We need more information and should read about this painting. This painting, by a Spanish painter (no surprise there), happens to be a protest piece created in response to the 1937 bombing of an actual village in Spain called Guernica where many civilians perished during the Spanish Civil War. Hmmmm, a deeper meaning seems to be coalescing. Meanwhile, what does all this mean back in St. Louis?

Aha! Tom has just alluded to: a rather infamous bombing, the Spanish Civil War itself, and the year 1937 all at once. Therefore we know the action of the play must be taking place after, or in reasonable proximity, to late April 1937 at the earliest. We now have a contextual clue to the setting and timeframe of Williams's play. We also now must consider the themes of war, protest, and violence while continuing to read, and these will become evident within the Wingfield household itself as the play unfolds. Tom isn't really talking about Spain at all, much less a painting. He's foreshadowing the family conflict to come.

Of course, we don't know any of this in the moment. The important thing to remember is that the significance of an allusion is very difficult to detect while reading. The pieces often fall into place later. Students often ask: how do we even know to look for allusions when we might not actually recognize them? The answer is to be on the lookout for them all the time. And when we come across words, vocabulary, or names of things we don't know . . . we should look them up! Be a proactive reader. Who knows where it will lead?

Here are several strategies for deciphering allusions in literature:

1. Are there proper nouns that you do not recognize or cannot identify? That proper noun might point the way to an allusion.

2. Can you establish the big idea or concept that the author wants to explain or illustrate by making the allusion? (Look at the sentences around the allusion to find the big idea.)

3. Does the allusion pertain to art, history, geography, politics, or popular culture?

4. If the allusion is artistic:
   a. Is it part of an art movement?
   b. Is it reactionary art?
   c. Is it protest art?
   d. What does the art mean to the story at hand?

5. If the allusion is historical:
   a. What happened?
   b. Where did it happen?
   c. When did it happen?
   d. Who was involved?
   e. What does this historical perspective mean to the story at hand?

6. If the allusion is geographical:
   a. Where in the world?
   b. Why is the location important?
   c. What does this location mean to the story at hand?

7. If the allusion is political:
   a. What views are expressed?
   b. Is the allusion pro or anti?
   c. Does it indicate direction or resolution for the story?
   d. What does this position mean to the story at hand?

8. If the allusion is from popular culture:
   a. Is it a movie?
   b. Is it a song?
   c. Is it a landmark film, novel, or person?
   d. What does this title or person mean to the story at hand?

Clearly you do not have to ask all of these questions when you are interrogating the allusion but this is a guide to your interrogation. Other questions may arise as you examine the allusion.

Derek Martin, English Teacher, Gill St. Bernard's School, 2014

# Workshop 13

## *Student Handout #2: Interrogating a Work of Art*

### Description

1. Who created the work of art?

2. Who ordered or commissioned the piece of art, if anyone?

3. What year was it created?

4. What medium was it created with (oil on canvas, stone sculpture, graphite drawing on paper, etc.)?

5. Where is it located?

6. What is the subject matter (name the objects you can identify: people, places things)?

7. Describe the elements of art you see in this piece of art:

    a.  What types of lines do you see (straight, curvy, sharp, intersecting, etc.)?

    b.  What types of shapes do you see (organic or geometric)?

    c.  What types of color or value (light, dark, warm, cool)?

    d.  What type of space (deep, shallow, linear perspective, overlapping, size differences)?

    e.  What types of texture (actual or implied, rough, smooth)?

### Analysis

1. How is the work organized?

2. Has the artist created **rhythm** in the work? Are there repeated elements or patterns that create a sense of rhythm?

3. How has the artist created a sense of **movement**? Has the artist drawn your attention to a focal point in the composition? How?

4. What type of **balance** is shown (symmetrical, radial, asymmetrical)?

5. How has the artist shown **contrast**? By opposing visual elements, size, or color?

6. How has the artist shown **emphasis**? Is something larger than other things? Brighter or bolder?

7. How has the artist created a sense of **unity**? Are there similar repeated shapes, colors, or marks?

## Interpretation

1. What is the mood or meaning of the work?

2. What is the artist trying to say?

3. Is the art work about a known story?

4. What does the piece remind you of?

5. Pretend you are inside this piece. What does it feel like?

6. Why do you suppose the artist made this painting?


## Judgment

1. What do you think of the work?

2. What do you think is good about this work?

3. What do you think is not so good?

4. Why do you think other people should see this work of art?

5. What do you think is worth remembering about this work?

These questions are for your use as you interrogate a specific piece of art. You may use some of them or all of them depending upon what you are thinking about your source. When you interrogate the piece of art some of your own questions will be raised and will be as valid as these questions.

Sarah Isusi, Fine Arts Teacher, Gill St. Bernard's, 2014

# Workshop 13

## *Student Handout #3: Interrogating a Coin or Pottery Sherd*

An item that depicts some authentic society or culture and that may have historical significance is sometimes called *realia*. That item represents the reality of the subject being studied. In archeology which studies artifacts of ancient cultures, coins and pottery sherds are two kinds of realia. They are authentic objects. Other authentic objects may also be interrogated in this same manner.

1. What is the object's material?
   a. Is it a natural object that has been modified?
   b. Is it man-made? Make note of color, texture, shape.
2. What is the size and shape of the object?
   a. Is the object complete or broken?
   b. In what way was it broken?
   c. Do you have other pieces of the same object?
   d. Can you piece it together?
3. What is the object's overall condition?
   a. Has the object been modified?
   b. Is its condition affected by its material? (i.e., rust, corrosion, fading)
4. Is the object "readable"?
   a. Is there an image on the object?
   b. Are there letters, words, or symbols?
   c. What do these tell you?
5. Where was the object found?
   a. Who made the object?
   b. When was the object made?
6. Was the object found alone?
   a. How did it get there?
   b. Why was it found there?
7. Were similar objects found together?
   a. What were the similar objects?
   b. What was their condition?
8. What do you know about the object's use?
   a. Who used this object?
   b. Were there any secondary uses?

9. In what environment was the object found?

    a. In sand or desert?

    b. In a riverbank?

    c. In a mound?

    d. In a field?

    e. Around or under a structure?

10. Could you trace the object to a specific social class (rich or poor, luxurious or utilitarian, etc.)?

These are some questions you may ask. You may ask other questions of your archaeological subjects depending upon what comes to mind as you are observing and interrogating the object.

Jennifer Diamond, Latin Teacher, Gill St. Bernard's, 2014

# Workshop 13

## *Student Handout #4: Interrogating Realistic Fiction*

### Objective Background Information

1. Who wrote the story?

2. Where is the author from?

3. When was it written?

4. Where is the story set: time, place?

5. What is the story generally about (do not summarize plot)?

6. What do you notice about its structure?

   a. Length of paragraphs?

   b. Types of sentences?

   c. What kind of diction?

   d. What kind of punctuation?

   e. Dialogue: excessive, sparse, terse?

   f. Does any imagery stand out?

   g. Verb tense?

   h. Type of narrator?

7. Are there any noticeable stylistic techniques used: italics, stream of consciousness, interior monologue, lack or excessive use of any part of speech?

8. What kind of characters are there? What are their attitudes?

9. Do any symbols or metaphors stand out?

### Analysis and Interpretation

1. Are there any shifts in the story? Voice? Verb tense? Chronology?

2. How does the story make you feel?

3. Do you sympathize with the characters?

4. What is the story's tone?

5. How does any element of structure help the story create meaning or make a point? For example, why are paragraphs so long? Why does the writer use so many italics? Why so many symbols?

6. What does the story's title communicate to you about the story? Is it only literal?

7. What is the author trying to communicate about the topic or subject of the story?

8. What is the author's main point?

Regardless of whether you are interrogating a novel, a short story, or a one page fictional essay, all or some of these questions may be used. Your reading of the fictional work may raise other questions that can become a part of the interrogation of the work.

Dr. Andrew Lutz, English Department Chair, Gill St. Bernard's, 2014

# Workshop 13

## *Student Handout #5: Interrogating a Garment*

There are three factors of a garment that contribute to understanding the garment. The three factors are: material, function, and decoration.

### Material Questions

1. What kind of a garment is this?
2. What is the age of the garment?
3. What color is the garment?
4. What is the garment made of?
    a. Is the textile (material) made of natural fibers (cotton, silk, wool, linen, fur)?
    b. Is the textile made of synthetic (man-made) fibers (acetate, polyester, faux fur)?
5. Is the garment manufactured?
6. If so, does the garment have a manufacturing tag?
7. Is the garment hand sewn?
8. Is the garment homemade?
9. If the fabric has a pattern, is the fabric printed or woven?
10. Is the garment in good, fair, or poor condition?

### Function Questions

1. Who is the wearer of the garment?
2. Is the garment a contemporary piece?
3. Does the garment come from a different time period? What period?
4. Does the garment indicate social status? How?
5. Does the garment indicate religious identity? How?
6. Does the garment indicate ethnicity? How?
7. Does the garment indicate gender identity? How?
8. Does the garment indicate the type of work of the wearer? (Example: carpenter's apron, ballet dancer's shoes, soldier's helmet?)
9. Is the garment used for utilitarian purposes (example: a police officer's vest for protection)?
10. Does the garment protect from the elements? How?
11. Is the garment used for work or play?
12. Is the garment used for formal or informal wear? Describe the occasion of its use, when the person would wear it or what activity the garment would be used for.
13. If the wearer changes the garment, does the status of the wearer change?

## Decorative Questions

1. Does the color of the garment indicate the situation or function of the wearer (example: a purple cape of a king?)

2. Does the color of the garment indicate an ethnic, cultural, religious, or social identity (example: a red bridal gown on a Chinese bride)?

3. What does the color represent?

4. Why is the wearer of the garment in that situation?

5. What circumstances led to that situation?

6. Does the garment have any decoration or adornment (beading, fabric trim, lace, applique, ribbon)? Describe the decoration. What does the decoration say about the garment?

7. Does the garment have closures (zipper, buttons, snaps, grommet, hook and eye, laces)? What do the closures say about the identity of the wearer? (Example: Amish people are not allowed to wear button closures on their clothes.)

You may ask all or some of the questions listed above. You may also think of other questions to interrogate the garment.

Paul Canada, Theatre Teacher, Gill St. Bernard's School, 2014

# Workshop 13

## *Student Handout #6: Interrogating a Graph*

A graph is a visual representation of a set of data or the relationship between two sets of data.

1. What is the title of the graph?

2. What type of graph is it? (Example: bar graph, scattered plot, line graph, etc.)

3. What does the horizontal axis measure? What do the numbers represent?

4. If the measurement is numerical, what is its scale? (Example: What is the numerical jump between units of measurement?)

5. What does the vertical axis measure?

6. What is the vertical axis scale?

7. What is the trend of the graph?

8. What does this tell you about the relationship between the two measures?

9. If there is more than one group of data shown on the graph or trend or patterns, how are they the same? How are they different?

10. Is the indicated trend (or trends) likely to continue? Why or why not?

11. How can you summarize in words what the graph shows?

You may use some or all of the questions indicated or create your own questions as you look at and work with the information in the graphs.

Cynthia Orr, Math Instructor, Gill St. Bernard's School, 2014

# Workshop 13

## Student Handout #7: Interrogating in an Interview

Often a researcher will locate a primary source who is willing to be interviewed, and such an interview can take place either face-to-face, by telephone, video chat, or e-mail. In any case, an interview focuses on a key element or elements of the research project and how the interviewee's information is placed within this project.

If you record audio or video of the interview, you must ask permission of the interviewee.

The questions below constitute some, though not all, of the questions you may ask in the interview. Unlike other types of sources, which are for the most part inanimate objects (both textual and nontextual), when you interrogate (ask questions of) your interviewee, remember to be sensitive to the fact that you are interviewing a human being. Thus, be polite, be organized, and be brief in your questions. And above all, take notes of both the verbal and nonverbal communication being relayed to you.

### Questions for an Interview

1. What is your name, title, and/or organizational identity?
2. What is your relationship with the topic?
3. How long have you been involved with the topic?
4. Why did you get involved with the topic?
5. What important feature or story can you tell me about the topic as you know it?
6. I am particularly interested in _____ (aspect) about the topic of my research. Can you give me more information about that?
7. I am also interested in _____ (another aspect). Can you tell me something about that aspect?
8. In my research, I have not been able to find too much information about _____. Is there anything you can tell me?
9. Are there any other resources I should look at about this topic?
10. Is there anything else you would like to add?

Other questions may arise during this interview. Ask them!

Your interview should be followed by a thank-you note to the person you interviewed. Your interview should be dated and identified by the method of the interview (personal, telephone, video conference, or e-mail).

When you take notes during your interview each item question asked should be transcribed into your notes with the answer following immediately. Use quotations for the answers as much as possible in your notes.

Amy Mai Tierney, Gill St. Bernard's School, 2014
Randell K. Schmidt, Gill St. Bernard's School, 2014

# Workshop 13

## *Student Handout #8: Interrogating a Legal Document*

1. What kind of legal document is it?

   a. Government bill

   b. Supreme Court verdict

   c. Paragraph of law (Section of the legal document)

   d. Treaty

   e. Religious stricture

2. Who wrote the text?

   a. Congress

   b. Court

   c. Authority

   d. University or educational institution

   e. Nation/State

   f. Religious entity (e.g., Catholic doctrine from the Vatican, Sharia law of Islam, Jewish law)

3. Who is the writer of the text and what is his authority?

4. What is the publication date of the law?

5. What is the legal issue (or social, political, economic issue) that the legal document addresses?

6. What are the main contents of the document?

7. Is this the first law of its kind or is it a revision of another law?

8. What is the meaning of the most important legal concept(s) of the text?

9. Is the text openly favoring specific views, favoring specific views in a hidden way, or is the text balanced?

10. Is the message of the document very clear or is the text open for different interpretations?

Any legal matter that is embodied in a legal document usually has a story behind it. It could be a family story (as in a will), a sociopolitical story (as in a law), or it could be a commercial/economic story (as in a treaty). The questions above should answer what kind of a story is behind the document. However, your reading of the document will raise other questions for you to further interrogate the document.

Goran Brolund, Extended Essay Instructor, Fyrisskolan Uppsala, Sweden

## Workshop 13

### *Student Handout #9: Interrogating a Live or Recorded Musical Performance*

A musical performance is one or more musicians playing and/or singing a musical piece. When one attends a live musical performance, listens to an audio recording of a musical performance, or views a video recording of a musical performance, some basic questions come to mind.

1. What is the title of the piece?
2. Who wrote it? When?
3. Who performed it? When? Where?
4. Did you see or hear a live performance, a video recording, or an audio recording?
5. What instruments were used?
6. Were the musicians professional (paid) or amateur (volunteer, student, etc.)?
7. What sorts of technology were involved in the performance? (Example: amplifiers, soundboard, computers, foot pedals, microphones, etc.)
8. Did the piece include singing? If so,
   a. What do the lyrics reveal about the song?
   b. Do the lyrics have a particular rhyme scheme?
   c. Do the lyrics tell the story or describe an event or feeling?
   d. What language are the lyrics in?
   e. Are there repeated sections of lyrics? If so, what was the songwriter's intention?
9. Was the song written or performed for a specific purpose (a holiday, a special event such as a wedding or graduation, to honor someone's memory, a worship service, a character song in a musical, etc.)?
10. Are there repeated elements in the song, such as a chorus or a certain melody or theme?
11. How would you describe the tempo (speed) of the song?
    a. Fast?
    b. Slow?
    c. Moderate?
    d. Varied?
12. Was the piece trying to portray any moods or emotions?
13. Was silence (even momentary or brief) part of the piece?
14. Did the piece include anything surprising or was it predictable?
15. How did the audience respond to the performance?
16. How did the audience response affect your own experience?

You may ask all of these questions or some of these questions to help you understand the musical piece. You may also ask some other questions to interrogate the musical piece.

David Southerland, Upper School Music Director, Gill St. Bernard's School, 2014

# Workshop 13

## *Student Handout #10: Interrogating a Natural Phenomenon*

Properly interpreting a natural phenomenon requires of the researcher a number of careful considerations. Many of these considerations are basic to all examinations:

1. What is the commonly accepted definition of the phenomenon? (Example: What is an earthquake? A comet? A radioactive nuclear decay?)
2. When and where did the event in question occur?
3. What were the conditions surrounding the event?
4. What were its sensory characteristics? (visual, auditory, etc.)
5. What is the historical significance of the event? Did the phenomenon support the prevailing view of the subject or did it cause a change in the way the phenomenon was interpreted?
6. Are there comparable events that must be considered or was the event unique?
7. Are there differences between seemingly comparable events?
8. To what extent is the observation dependent on the observer?

This last question is of vital importance in the proper interpretation and analysis of a natural phenomenon. In particular, a differentiation must be made between a direct observation of an event by the researcher, as opposed to the report of an event by some other individual or group. In the latter situation, a number of variables must be considered:

1. Above all, how reliable is the source? Has the source been peer-reviewed or supported by an outside authority, or is this an independently reported examination of an event?
2. What were the methods employed by the source to acquire the data they present? Were the methods used part of a commonly accepted practice, or were they in some way controversial or part of a unique protocol?
3. What instruments were used in the examination?
4. To what extent were issues of experimental error and/or bias addressed?
5. Were assumptions made in the interpretation of the data, and if so, how logical were the assumptions?

If, on the other hand, the report of a phenomenon is based directly on a researcher's observations, the following must be considered:

1. How confident is the observer that the data he collected will be objective (unbiased by expectations or false assumptions) and comprehensive?
2. How skilled is he in observational techniques?
3. What tools were employed in the examination? Were they reasonably chosen? Did they yield an undistorted view of the phenomenon?

Finally, one last question must be asked by the researcher when examining any natural event or occurrence: "Why?" Why did this volcano erupt as it did? Why was a neutrino released by this particular nuclear decay? Why is the sky blue? Such an investigation of the causal links surrounding an event is of vital importance for any competent and complete analysis. It is, indeed, the basis of all scientific inquiry.

Laurence Bostian, Physics Teacher, Gill St. Bernard's, 2014

# Workshop 13

## *Student Handout #11: Interrogating a Textual Source of Nonfiction*

A textual source of nonfiction is usually considered a collection of information or data expressed and held in written, often edited forms. Much of the text used in the humanities is work that has been printed and published to be distributed and read. But as social media gains more traction in the scholarly world, some text has not been edited and/or has been self-published. Such "raw" text is like a primary source—such as an unpublished diary, ledger, or cookbook—a free-standing work that should be acknowledged as such.

When a nonfiction text is used for a source, the researcher may direct the following questions to it:

1. What is the title of the text?
2. What is the nature of the text?
   a. It is a speech text?
   b. It is a memoir?
   c. Is it an historical text?
   d. Is it a piece of social criticism or a review?
   e. Is it a humorous or satirical piece?
   f. Is it a guide or a "how to" text?
3. What is the central message of the text?
4. Who was the author?
5. If no one is named as author, who was the editor?
6. Why was the text written?
7. When was it written and published?
8. Who was the publisher?
9. Who is the intended audience?
10. Are there illustrations in the text?
11. What do the illustrations show about the text?
12. What type of illustrations are they?
    a. Photo
    b. Drawing
    c. Cartoon
    d. Painting
    e. Chart or graph
13. Is the work able to convey the subject as stated in the title of the work?
14. How well is the subject conveyed?
15. What is missing from the work?
16. Why is it missing from the work?

These are some questions to use when interrogating textual nonfiction materials. Certainly other questions will arise as you read the text, and when you ask these questions you may find some of them do not pertain to your research. Use what you wish to use and make notes of the answers to your questions.

Lee Fitzgerald, Charles Sturt College, Australia, 2014
Randell K. Schmidt, Gill St. Bernard's School, 2014

# Workshop 13

## *Student Handout #12: Interrogating a Photograph*

1. Who took the photograph?
2. When was the photograph taken?
3. What is being photographed (subject of photograph)?
4. Describe the composition of the photograph
   a. Was it a planned event?
   b. Was it a chance event?
5. Was the photograph trying to capture a specific actor or action?
6. Was the photograph trying to capture an emotion or mood?
7. How did the lighting (light and shadow) or time of day affect the photo's message?
8. Is the photo a traditional shot, such as a pose or portrait, landscape, seascape, or figure?
9. Is the photo innovative in composition, detail, and/or texture?
10. Does the photo represent fantasy or reality?
11. Was the photo altered before it was printed?
    a. Was it digitally altered?
    b. Was other media added?
12. Does the photo tell a story?
    a. What is that story?
    b. Is the story one-sided?
    c. Is the photograph beneficial to every viewer or only to some?
13. Was the situation in the photograph arranged or did it occur naturally?
14. What is the social and/or historical context behind the photographer's motive?

These questions are some that you may use to examine and analyze the photograph. As you are examining the photograph you may find that some of these questions do not pertain to your research. It is important to know that you may formulate some other questions based upon your research and also upon your interrogation of the photograph. The questions above are guides for you. Use what you can and make notes on your answers.

Robert Ort, Photography Teacher, Gill St. Bernard's, 2014

## Workshop 13

### *Student Handout #13: Interrogating a Political Cartoon*

The following questions and ideas may assist you in organizing research around the interrogation of a political cartoon.

1. What is the title of the cartoon?
2. What is the cartoon's publication date?
3. Who is the publisher?
4. Who is the cartoonist?
5. Is there additional relevant information about the cartoon (usually provided at the bottom of the cartoon)?
6. In what publication did the cartoon appear (name the newspaper, book, magazine, or broadside)?
7. What is the subject of the cartoon? In other words, what was the cartoon drawn to portray?
8. What or who does the cartoon target? A political party, organization, figure, or action?
9. How does the subject of the cartoon relate to an historical context? Describe it.
10. Is there a protagonist, that is, someone forcing the action in the cartoon?
11. Is there an attitude in a character or other element of the cartoon that conveys a particular viewpoint?
12. How is this attitude or element portrayed?
13. Does the cartoon seem to have a bias or propagandist edge?
14. How does the cartoon reflect this bias?
15. What is your complete interpretation of the cartoon in its political and historical context?
16. Does your interpretation affect how you look at other information from the same historical period?
17. Is the cartoon effective? Why?
18. Did you learn something about your own biases through this kind of cartoon?
19. After interrogating the cartoon did you return to other sources of information with a different viewpoint or understanding?
20. Does the cartoon convey information that illuminates other information sources you have used?
21. Is the message clearer in this format than a traditional text? Does it attract more of your interest and attention?

Political cartoons are very useful in promoting exchange of ideas in which you share your knowledge and skills. Everyone learns together.

Dr. John Ripton, History Department Chair, Gill St. Bernard's, 2014

# Workshop 13

## *Student Handout #14: Interrogating a Live or Recorded Speech, or a Transcript of a Speech*

1. Who is delivering the speech?

2. What is the speaker's title, position, and professional and personal characteristics?

3. Is the purpose of the speech known?

4. In what setting is the speech delivered?

    a. Inside/ outside

    b. Weather

    c. Type of venue

    d. Size of audience

    e. Type of audience

5. Who else is on stage or near the speaker?

6. Can you identify the background or the context for why the speech is being delivered (such as State of the Union, memorial service, or commencement)?

7. Does that context affect the message of the speech?

8. Can you observe any clues that would describe the emotional state of the speaker? Audience?

9. Describe the tone of the speech (i.e., happy, somber, angry, or determined)?

10. What is the central message being delivered in the speech?

11. Why is that message being delivered?

12. List any main points of emphasis from the speech.

13. Are there visual aids for the audience? What information do the visual aids provide?

14. Does the speaker use prompts, notes, or does the speaker deliver the speech extemporaneously (i.e., spontaneously without notes)?

15. How does the audience receive the speech? Chart their feedback (i.e., applause, laughter, boos, cheers and at what point in the speech do those reactions occur?).

16. Does the reaction of the audience give you any clues as to the characteristics of the audience members?

17. Describe the body language of the speaker. Does it aid or hinder the speech?

18. List any concepts or vocabulary words that you hear in the speech, but that you do not understand.

19. Did the speech make you feel any emotions? Describe how you felt.

20. What is your response to the speech (agreement or disagreement, belief or disbelief, surprised or bored, captivated, inspired, moved or disgusted, offended, etc.)?

21. Did the speech give you a better understanding of the topic at hand? What is the new understanding?

These are some questions you may use to interrogate the speech that you have chosen as a source. You do not have to use all of these questions and you may also think of other questions to ask about the speech, its delivery, and the response it gets.

William Diamond, History Teacher, Gill St. Bernard's, 2014

# Workshop 13

## *Student Handout #15: Interrogating of a Live or Recorded Sporting Event*

1. What teams or individuals are participating in the sporting event?

2. When is the date of the sporting event?

3. Where is the location of the sporting event?

4. What is the setting for the sporting event?

    a. Inside/Outside

    b. Weather

    c. Venue

    d. Size of audience

    e. Home game for one team or neutral site?

5. What is the context for this sporting event?

    a. Regular season

    b. Playoffs? What round?

    c. Major rivalry

    d. David vs. Goliath contest

    e. Rematch

6. If it is a historical sporting event, how do the equipment and uniforms differ from present-day gear? Does that impact the game?

7. If the sporting event is recorded, who are the commentators?

8. Who are the best players on the teams?

9. Which players play a key role in this particular sporting event?

10. Describe the flow of the sporting event. An early lead for one team? Tight match with a late score? Domination by one team?

11. Describe an important play or plays that impacted the outcome of the sporting event.

12. What was the response of the crowd/attendees?

13. What was the final result of the sporting event?

14. What is the next step for the winner?

Kristen Armstrong, Soccer Coach and Librarian, Gill St. Bernard's School, 2014

## Workshop 13

### *Student Handout #16: Interrogating a Live or Recorded Theater Performance*

A theatrical performance utilizes three devices to create the experience between stage actors and theatergoers. These devices are visual, audio, and character development. When one is viewing a performance some basic questions come to mind. Look at the playbill or the credits for assistance in your interrogation.

You will ask some authority questions about the play.

1. What is the name of the play?
2. Who wrote the play?
3. Who directed the play?
4. Who are the main actors?

You will ask some visual questions about the performance:

1. In what time period does the play take place?
2. Is it a formal performance with the audience watching and the actors acting?
3. Is it an interactive performance where the audience is part of the play?
4. What role does the lighting of the stage serve in the performance?
5. What does the scenery do?
6. Do the backdrop and the props help you understand the play? And why?
7. What does the costuming (what the actors are wearing) tell you about the characters in the play?
8. Can you understand the social economic roles of the characters by their costumes (rich or poor, educated or not, working class or ruling class, age, job situation, and health)?

You will ask some audio questions about the performance:

1. Is music part of the play? If so, what kind of music?
2. Is the play a musical, meaning that the story is told in song?
3. Is the language used by the actors a modern language, Shakespearean verse, rhyme verse, or an ancient language?
4. Are the actors using dialects that are not standard English? Do you know where the dialect is from?
5. How is silence used? Does silence create a feeling of conflict or unrest?

You will ask some questions about character development:

1. The main character(s) is called a protagonist, hero, or heroine. Does that character(s) get what he wants by the end of the play?
2. What does the protagonist have to achieve to get what he wants?
3. How does the protagonist overcome the barriers?
4. Is there an evil one in the play? What is the role of the evil one?

These questions are some questions that you may use to examine and analyze the performance. As you are interrogating the performance you may find that some of these questions do not pertain to your research. It is important to know that you may formulate some other questions based upon your research and also upon your interrogation of the performance. These questions are guides for you. Use what you can and make notes on your answers to the questions.

Margery Schiesswohl, Drama Teacher, Gill St. Bernard's School, 2014

## Workshop 14

### Overview: Further Developing the Research Question into a Thesis Using Ideas Uncovered While Interrogating the Sources

The student is now deep in the formulation stage, taking the new information and beginning to focus attention on certain aspects, ideas, or factors about his research topic. The goal of this workshop is the student's formulation and articulation of a more fully stated research question based upon the new information the student has gained from handling his various information sources, either by reading, viewing, hearing, or interacting through interrogation with the source. Such interrogations direct the student's attention to the actual content of the source and place that content in a context which then lends deeper meaning to the content. Such interrogations provide opportunities for the student to learn more about his research subject and to build a broader base of knowledge, which then can be used to further develop and more clearly articulate his research question.

Having completed the interrogation of approximately two-thirds of his sources, the student is now able to characterize his topic with descriptions and examples of actions done by or to his topic. The student's research has provided those descriptions and actions and should have provoked some changes in what the student thinks about and knows about his topic. Those changes in thinking are good! The research process is, after all, a chance to think differently about a topic.

So, if the student has briefly summarized his notes from each source he has interrogated, patterns of information may appear and certainly ideas he did not previously have may come to mind about his topic. And, in fact, other questions that he did not initially have may now be surfacing. These new questions, ideas, and patterns lend themselves to formulating a more sophisticated research question, one that the student's research has already helped him to begin to answer.

In some cases his new knowledge may radically alter his research question, but more often the new knowledge will lend more detail and depth to his existing simple research question, leading more toward the development of the statement (a thesis) that responds to or answers at least somewhat his research question. Thus, the neophyte humanities researcher, who frankly began the research project knowing too little, asks a substantive research question about his topic. Left alone to formulate an information-based thesis, he has now arrived at the point where his simple curiosity about a subject can be articulated into a more informed research question. His information search has yielded enough information to produce questions in his mind. He is moving from ignorance to information processing to some original ideas and hopefully, newer questions. Isn't research grand?

All of the above said, the teachers and librarians should be attentive now. Students may not clearly or easily articulate what they have learned. Private one-on-one conversations with each student researcher may be called for. Or, an exercise may be undertaken in which study buddies discuss with each other the findings of their newly completed research of their three to five sources. Study buddies will inform each other of patterns, ideas, and questions these sources have introduced to the student researcher. Peer feedback from the study buddies eliminates perceived pressures from adult guides for the student who is yet uneasy about his own efforts. Such peer feedback can be accomplished at the reflection phase of the workshop time as students share their work with one or two other students.

At this stage, the workshop focuses on fully developing the research question by examining the notes made while handling and interrogating the sources. **Handout #1: Further Developing the Research Question Using Your Notes** should be given to the students at the start of the workshop. The workshop should take place in an area with plenty of space to spread out the student's work.

## Workshop 14: Further Developing the Research Question into a Thesis Using Ideas Uncovered While Interrogating the Sources

**Learning Goals:** The goal of this workshop is the student's formulation and articulation of a more fully stated research question based upon the new information gained from the sources.

**Location:** Classroom

**Team:** Teacher, librarian, and assistant teacher or librarian

**Inquiry Unit:** In this workshop the student formulates a more detailed and specific research question. This question will aid him in later organizing his research notes and eventually result in a cogent research thesis for his paper, as patterns, big ideas, and other questions present themselves in his research notes.

**Total Time:** 50 minutes

| **Starter**<br>Time: 5 minutes<br><br>Inquiry<br>Community | Teacher and librarian pass out blank sheets of paper and ask the students to get out their research notes. Students are informed that today they will formulate a more developed research question. **Handout #1: Further Developing the Research Question Using Your Notes** is distributed and read aloud by students. |
|---|---|
| **Work Time**<br>Time: 40 minutes<br><br>Individual Student<br>Researcher | Students take their notes and, following the instructions in the handout, begin to read their notes and mark them, looking for patterns of similar topic information, a recurring big idea or theme, factors that are repeated in several notes, or characteristics that appear in more than one source.<br><br>A student should take the blank sheet and begin to list such patterns, factors, big ideas, or characteristics they find in the notes. This list should yield three or more subtopics that fall under the general research topic and more fully explain or illustrate in greater depth the research question. This list will enable the student researcher to reframe his simple research question, incorporating three (because generally the paper requires three) aspects of the subject that his research has uncovered into a more articulate research question. **Note: The student should be reminded now that he will not necessarily use all of his notes as he completes his paper.**<br><br>Now, once that question is formed the student can use his research notes to formulate a research thesis. Taking his developed question with the three identified aspects of his subject, he can weave his question into a research statement (thesis).<br><br>The thesis basically answers his more developed research question using the evidence indicated in his notes about the three factors, patterns, big ideas, or characteristics found in his sources. |

| **Reflection**<br>Time: 5 minutes<br><br>Study Buddies | Study buddies share research findings and critique each other's more developed research question which will lead to a potential research thesis. |
|---|---|
| **Notes:** | This workshop is complex and laborious. Students may need a second unstructured workshop period to complete the research question and begin the thesis statement. Teacher and librarian should be circulating constantly and assisting those students in need of intervention.<br><br>Students should be informed that the next workshop will concentrate on organizing their notes to prepare to make an outline of the research. They absolutely must bring all borrowed information notes to class. |
| **Common Core Standards:** | CCSS.ELA-LITERACY.W.9-10.2.A<br>Introduce a topic; organize complex ideas, concepts, and information to make important connections and distinctions; include formatting (e.g., headings), graphics (e.g., figures, tables), and multimedia when useful to aiding comprehension.<br><br>CCSS.ELA-LITERACY.W.9-10.5<br>Develop and strengthen writing as needed by planning, revising, editing, rewriting, or trying a new approach, focusing on addressing what is most significant for a specific purpose and audience. (Editing for conventions should demonstrate command of Language standards 1–3 up to and including grades 9–10 here.) |

# Workshop 14

## *Student Handout #1: Further Developing the Research Question Using Your Notes*

1. Take out a blank sheet of paper and on it write down your simple research question.

2. Let us now focus on further developing your research question. Read the notes that you now have and, using the blank sheet of paper with your question on it, read and process your notes.

3. As you read your notes, you can begin to code them with colored marker, alphabetical letters, or identifying words at the top right-hand corner of the note. As you are reading, notice patterns, factors, big ideas, or characteristics that appear in more than one or two notes and sources. On the blank sheet of paper, name the patterns, characteristics, or big ideas as you interpret them.

   *For example, the content of your note about Theodor Geisel's (Dr. Seuss) work* The Lorax *might be coded by you as environmentalism, while the word "environmentalism" is not actually in the note itself.* You are reading between the lines! You are depicting a big idea the note is about.

   Please remember, many of your notes are all about what the cultural critics are saying about the work and the influence of the creator of the work. That is what you are interpreting.

4. Once you have an informal list of patterns, factors, big ideas, or characteristics, try to discern three specific categories that you might fashion into a more detailed research question. The detailed research question becomes a more evolved question than the simple question on the top of your page. **If you are having trouble, ask the teacher or librarian for help.**

5. Now, as the question becomes more articulated and the three concepts are identified, each concept (body of evidence from your information) can support the answer to your question. So, by incorporating each of the three bodies of evidence to answer your question you can turn the question into a strong statement about your research (otherwise known as the thesis). In other words, your thesis indicates the "big" findings of your research—as you interpret them.

Your Thesis:

_____

_____

_____

# Research in the Collection Stage of the Information Search Process

Workshop 15: How to Organize Your Borrowed Information into an Outline
Workshop 16: Filling the Research Holes

In the Collection Stage, the student continues to focus on the research question and developing a thesis. He begins to organize what information he has already to determine what else he needs that is pertinent to the support he is building for his thesis. The documentation he seeks is particular and more easily recognizable to the researcher.

In the Collection Stage student confidence builds as the student takes full control of his project. However, the teacher and librarian may need to assist some students in finding more pertinent information to identify and fill the research holes. Therefore, the workshops are designed to begin filling the research holes.

# Workshop 15

## Overview: How to Organize Your Borrowed Information into an Outline

The goal of this workshop is the introduction of three distinct methods to organize notes for the purpose of presenting the findings of the research in paper or presentation form. All three methods require review of notes, categorization of information held in notes, some organizing action, and finally the synthesis of multiple notes from varied sources to **create a *unique-to-each-student* statement of findings in the research as well as the critical and analytical response of the student to the findings.** Depending upon the researcher's learning style(s) and prior academic preparation for this extensive project, a teacher may choose to teach one of these methods to organize the information or teach all methods and allow students to choose the one he feels suits his style best.

A brief description of each method is included here and in the student **Handout #1: How to Organize Your Borrowed Information into an Outline** for this workshop. The workshop itself is a hands-on period for students, to begin organizing their notes. Students should also receive **Handout #2: Making an Outline** to begin that task once the notes are organized.

### Organizing Notes: A

1. All notes, either handwritten or digitally printed, should be divided into distinct single entities. In other words, if the student has 100 notes, each one should be on a single slip of paper or notecard.

2. The student should read each note and signify with a word or two (on top of the note) what the note is about—what category or topic the note discusses.

3. Similar notes (meaning notes with the same or similar categories) should be placed in a pile. Distinct piles indicate distinct and separate categories. These categories become the major sections or subtopics of the outline for the paper or presentation. As the student conducts the research he may come to realize what these subtopics are. Or he may not realize them until he actually starts putting his notes in distinct piles.

4. Once the different subtopics of the paper are identified for a basic outline, the student can further arrange each distinct pile of notes for sub-subtopics or simply place the notes in the sequence he can best present them; trying to utilize different sources and information from the notes that he pieced together provides a broader picture or more details about his research thesis.

### Organizing Notes: B

1. All notes, either handwritten or digitally produced and either held individually or in a notebook form, should be reviewed by the student by thoroughly reading each note and keeping a list of possible subtopics as the notes are reviewed.

2. During the review the student may mark the notes with different colored sticky notes or different colored highlighting to differentiate content. Thus, one subtopic might be pink, another might be blue, and so on.

3. After the review of the content, the student will determine the major subtopics of the notes and create a basic outline that can then be filled in by looking at the similarly colored notes and putting them into a sequence.

4. Any notes not utilized in the initial outline can be reviewed to determine whether they could be used along with other material that must be further researched or discarded.

## Organizing Notes: C

This method of organization is useful for the student who is having trouble finding the major categories of his notes and determining a basic organization pattern.

1. Gather all notes in one place and read through the notes.

2. Make a list of possible subtopics.

3. Make a chart, a web, or some graphic visualization of the different materials you have collected.

4. Determine the organization of your material by the creative or cultural work you are reviewing. Or,

5. Determine if you have three examples that answer your research question.

6. Organize materials by:

   a. Chronology

   b. Positive or negative arguments

   c. Changing cultural attitudes or values

   d. A shift in interpretation of the works

7. Consult with your teacher to determine the viability of the organization.

It is this practice of putting together information from multiple sources and (hopefully) more than one perspective with voices that may not agree, that provides the conditions for synthesis in the student's thinking and for newer ideas to be experienced by the student researcher.

Any of these methods may be tweaked or adapted to fit the research preparation level of the whole class or to respond to the educational needs of particular students. Other methods for organizing notes for presentation of a paper may also be used.

## Workshop 15: How to Organize Your Borrowed Information into an Outline

**Learning Goals:** The goal of this workshop is to use the notes of borrowed information to create the outline for presentation of the research.

**Location:** Library

**Team:** Librarian, teacher, and research aide

**Inquiry Unit:** In this unit in the collection stage, the student arranges his already borrowed information to determine the holes in his research so as to finish collecting information and complete the outline of the paper.

**Total Time:** 100 minutes (two workshop periods)

| | |
|---|---|
| **Starter**<br>Time: 15 minutes<br><br>Inquiry<br>Community | The librarian asks students if they are ready to begin organizing their borrowed information. Containers of colored highlighters or pens should be placed on research tables. **Handout #1: How to Organize Your Borrowed Information into an Outline** should be given to each student and read aloud by student volunteers. **Handout #2: Making an Outline** should also be distributed and read aloud. |
| **Work Time**<br>Time: 75 minutes<br><br>Individual<br>Scholars | During two work periods students will organize their notes to prepare to work on their outline. |
| **Reflection**<br>Time: 10 minutes<br><br>Study Buddies | Study buddies will discuss the progress made and problems encountered to assist one another in drafting the research outlines. |
| **Notes:** | In some classes, study buddy pairs may work together throughout the work time to help one another organize their notes. Because this workshop covers the two separate functions of organizing the notes and creating an outline, it could be taught as two distinctly separate workshops.<br><br>For all students, an additional unstructured workshop will be helpful to complete the draft outline.<br><br>The outline is a draft because most students will have gaps in their information and will have to collect more pertinent information to fill in the research holes and finalize their outline.<br><br>Plenty of space is needed to spread out notebooks and other materials while students are organizing their materials. |

| Common Core Standards: | CCSS.ELA-LITERACY.W.9-10.2.A<br>Introduce a topic; organize complex ideas, concepts, and information to make important connections and distinctions; include formatting (e.g., headings), graphics (e.g., figures, tables), and multimedia when useful to aiding comprehension.<br><br>CCSS.ELA-LITERACY.W.9-10.1.B<br>Develop claim(s) and counterclaims fairly, supplying evidence for each while pointing out the strengths and limitations of both in a manner that anticipates the audience's knowledge level and concerns. |
|---|---|

# Workshop 15

## *Student Handout #1: How to Organize Your Borrowed Information into an Outline*

Remember that you will be organizing your notes to provide an introduction that includes your thesis, three bodies of evidence that support your thesis, and finally your conclusion. Regardless of whether your notes are digitally recorded and held in a file or on paper or note cards, you must now consider each one separately to determine the contents. One way to determine the contents is to describe in a word or two the big idea or factor that your research has uncovered about your topic. When you determine the idea or factors mark the note with a color or notation. After all the notes have each been considered, begin to separate them and distinguish or identify three different bodies of evidence from those notes. You should now remember that each body of evidence, support, or explanation that you use should show three distinctly different sources and citations for a well-rounded research paper.

### Organizing Notes: A

1. All notes, either handwritten or digitally printed, should be divided into distinct single entities. In other words, if you have 100 notes, each one should be on a single slip of paper or notecard.

2. Read each note and signify with a word or two (on top of the note) what the note is about—what category or topic the note discusses.

3. Similar notes (meaning notes with the same or similar categories) should be placed in a pile. Distinct piles indicate distinct and separate categories. These categories become the major sections or subtopics of the outline for the paper or presentation. As you conducted the research you may have realized what these subtopics are, or you might not until you actually start to put your notes in distinct piles.

4. Once the different subtopics of the paper are identified for a basic outline, you can further arrange each distinct pile of notes for sub-subtopics or simply place the notes and number in the sequence you can best present them, trying to utilize different sources and information from the notes that you pieced together to provide a broader picture or more details about your research thesis.

### Organizing Notes: B

1. All notes, either handwritten or digitally produced and held individually or in a notebook form, should be reviewed by thoroughly reading each note and keeping a list of possible subtopics as the notes are reviewed.

2. During the review you may mark the notes with different colored sticky notes or different colored highlighting to differentiate content. Thus, one subtopic might be pink, another might be blue, and so on.

3. After the review of the content you will determine the major subtopics of the notes and create a basic outline that can then be filled in by looking at the similarly colored notes and organizing them into a sequence.

4. Any notes not utilized in the initial outline can be reviewed to determine whether to discard the note or to further research the information.

## Organizing Notes: C

This method of organization is useful for the student who is having trouble finding the major categories of his notes and determining a basic organization pattern.

1. Gather all notes in one place and read through the notes.
2. Make a list of possible subtopics.
3. Make a chart, a web, or some graphic visualization of the different materials you have collected.
4. Determine the organization of your material by the creative or cultural work you are reviewing. Or,
5. Determine if you have three examples that answer your research question.
6. Organize materials by:
    a. Chronology
    b. Positive or negative arguments
    c. Comparison and contrast
    d. Changing cultural attitudes or values
    e. A shift in interpretation of the works
7. Consult with your teacher to determine the viability of the organization.

Remember that you are going to use at least three distinct sources for each of your three bodies of evidence, and often you may use more than three sources.

# Workshop 15

## *Student Handout #2: Making an Outline*

An outline for a research paper provides a skeleton upon which the researcher hangs the evidence to show the reader whether the information he has found supports his thesis or negates it. A research paper contains four major parts after the title and heading.

I.    The first page holds the introduction, which includes the hook and your statement of thesis in some kind of context (historical, cultural, political, etc.).

II.   The body of the paper includes the evidence uncovered in the research with in-text citations.

    A.  First set of evidence (subtopic)

       1.  Sub-subtopic

       2.  Sub-subtopic

       3.  Sub-subtopic

       4.  Interpretation/analysis of evidence in A

    B.  Second set of evidence (subtopic)

       1.  Sub-subtopic

       2.  Sub-subtopic

       3.  Sub-subtopic

       4.  Interpretation/analysis of evidence in B

    C.  Third set of evidence (subtopic)

       1.  Sub-subtopic

       2.  Sub-subtopic

       3.  Sub-subtopic

       4.  Interpretation/analysis of evidence in C

III.  The conclusion of the paper provides the connection between the three bodies of evidence (A, B, C) and the statement of thesis. This reiterates what you have said in analyzing the three sets of evidence. The conclusion should be brief (2–3 paragraphs) and the only new information that should be added is suggestions for further research.

IV.   The MLA style Works Cited page(s) includes all cited materials.

# Workshop 16

## Overview: Filling the Research Holes

The goal of this workshop is to help the student identify gaps or holes in his information needed to support his thesis statement and begin to fill those holes.

By this point in the Collection Stage of the Information Search Process, the student has selected notes made from his sources and assembled an outline that is probably incomplete. All of this is to be expected. While he already has much information, he needs to fill in some holes or gaps where one or two of the bodies of evidence being used may be insufficient to fully support his thesis. As Kuhlthau's Information Search Process model shows, he must continue to look for more pertinent information that fits into and fills in his outline and thus gives more support to his thesis (Kuhlthau, 2004).

For some students, this task is not difficult as they are familiar enough with their already used sources to go back and find more information. Or they are confident enough searching to strategize and continue looking in other sources. However, occasionally a student will come to a standstill. For that student, the end of the research process appeared so close yet now seems very far away. Such a student can benefit from an intervention by the librarian who will point him in one of several directions:

1. Look deeper in the same sources.

2. Find a related source, perhaps by looking at the reference lists of already used sources.

3. Do some backdoor research in which "you are searching for unusual, exciting, or offbeat information about the research topic by following indirect search paths, i.e., 'stuff' indirectly related to the research topic—but 'stuff' interesting to the researcher" (Schmidt, 2013, 117).

4. Rethink the particular body of evidence (with the holes) to reframe it, restate it, or replace it as one of the three "proofs" of the thesis.

Obviously, any of these four directions to fill the holes will mean extending the time and effort needed to complete the Collection Stage prior to preparing the paper.

## Workshop 16: Filling the Research Holes

**Learning Goals:** The goal of this workshop is to help the student identify holes or gaps in the information needed to support his thesis.

**Location:** Library

**Team:** Teacher, librarian, and writing resource aide

**Inquiry Unit:** This workshop completes the Collection Stage of the Information Search Process and provides directions for solidifying the evidence to support the paper's thesis.

**Total Time:** 50 minutes

| | |
|---|---|
| **Starter**<br>Time: 10 minutes<br><br>Inquiry<br>Community | The librarian writes one question on the board and one statement. The question is, "Do you have three complete bodies of evidence for your paper?" The response is, "If you do, then refer to **Workshop 17: Writing the Paper, Handout #1.**"<br><br>However, for most students **Workshop 16: Filling the Research Holes** will provide alternatives to proceed with filling in the research holes. The librarian should determine the level(s) of help needed and divide the two groups. Those who only need to fill in one body of evidence should work in one group. Those who need to fill in more holes should work in another group with the writing aide who will be joined by the librarian later, when she has finished working with the first group.<br><br>Each student will receive **Handout # 1: Directions for Filling the Holes In Your Research.** The student scholar may use this handout to finish his research. The librarian should review and explain these four directions to the students in both groups using examples the students can relate to. |
| **Work Time**<br>Time: 35 minutes<br><br>Scholar Groups | Group I gathers with the librarian.<br>Group II gathers with the writing resource aide.<br><br>Each student identifies the gap(s) or hole(s) simply by reviewing his outline or looking at his collection of notes. The identified holes or gaps reduce the significance of the evidence and make the body of evidence skimpy or not understandable. Working with the guide, each student will choose one or more directions to follow up his previous research, identifying resources and beginning more note-taking. |
| **Reflection**<br>Time: 5 minutes<br><br>Inquiry<br>Community | Students should reflect on the degree of work completed and whether more work time is needed. |
| **Notes:** | One or two unstructured workshop times and/or individual tutoring sessions should be scheduled to assist students in completing their research and filling in the holes in their outlines. |

| Common Core Standards: | CCSS.ELA-LITERACY.WHST.9-10.2.B<br>Develop the topic with well-chosen, relevant, and sufficient facts, extended definitions, concrete details, quotations, or other information and examples appropriate to the audience's knowledge of the topic.<br><br>CCSS.ELA-LITERACY.WHST.9-10.5<br>Develop and strengthen writing as needed by planning, revising, editing, rewriting, or trying a new approach, focusing on addressing what is most significant for a specific purpose and audience.<br><br>CCSS.ELA-LITERACY.WHST.9-10.7<br>Conduct short as well as more sustained research projects to answer a question (including a self-generated question) or solve a problem; narrow or broaden the inquiry when appropriate; synthesize multiple sources on the subject, demonstrating understanding of the subject under investigation. |
|---|---|

# Workshop 16

## *Student Handout #1: Directions for Filling the Holes in Your Research*

A researcher often does not end up with three evenly distributed bodies of evidence to support the thesis and must return to a research position to fill in the holes.

1. Look deeper in the same sources:

   If it is a book, check the table of contents and index for more information. If it is a digitally held resource, fashion a more specific search term to search within the text. Read the captions of photographs or graphics.

2. Look for a related source by the same author, or by an author of another source from the works cited in your original sources. Check the digital library catalogue for similar resources under the same or similar call number.

3. Do some "backdoor" research. In backdoor research, the scholar focuses on some aspect of the research topic that is "unusual, exciting, or offbeat information about the research topic by following indirect search paths, i.e. 'stuff' indirectly related to the research topic—but 'stuff' interesting to the researcher" and pertinent to the body of evidence (Schmidt, 2013, 117).

4. Rethink your particular body of evidence that may seem skimpy. Try to reframe it, restate the concept, or replace the whole body of evidence as one of your three "proofs" of the thesis. Occasionally, a body of evidence cannot be easily improved, explained, or added to by the scholar. When this occurs, a major shift should be made. The student should return to his research notes and determine how to fashion some unused notes into a new body of evidence or even, perhaps, make new notes to create a new "third" body of evidence. This might require more research time to fill the holes.

# Research in the Presentation Stage of the Information Search Process

Workshop 17: Writing the Paper
Workshop 18: Writing a Conclusion and Creating a "Cover Page"
Workshop 19: Preparing to Peer Edit the Draft

In the Presentation Stage of the Information Search Process, the student prepares his information into a document which includes all the sections of his paper, from the "cover page" to the works cited page(s). The paper, which follows the MLA style, must meet all criteria of a standard humanities research paper.

At this point in the process, the teaching team should be available for individual consultation and, if possible, schedule additional unstructured workshop time for students to finish the paper—in all its glory!

Depending upon the work that each scholar accomplishes and the meaning that each scholar finds in his own research, individual students will express varying degrees of satisfaction or disappointment (see Kuhlthau's ISP model, page 7). All students, however, will express relief as they near the end of their efforts.

## Workshop 17

## Overview: Writing the Paper

The goal of this workshop is to demystify the process of writing the humanities research paper and to begin the actual writing of the paper. To initiate the process, a basic formulaic approach is provided to students. **The teacher and librarian may alter the formula specifically as it relates to the student's analysis statements.**

A formulaic approach for a 10-page paper in the humanities:

Page 1: The heading, the title, the page number, and the introduction incorporating the hook and the thesis (2–4 paragraphs). If there is still room on page 1 begin the exposition of the first body of evidence. If not, begin on page 2.

Page 2–4: In the exposition of the first body of evidence, the first at least two to four paragraphs will explain the overall nature of the first body of evidence and will usually be followed by three or four points describing, explaining, or providing more detail about the first body of evidence. In other words, these three points provide background and context that should be given in the body of evidence. Within each of the three bodies of evidence of the paper, the student should include some analysis statement(s) based upon his own growing knowledge and understanding of the subject.

Pages 5–7: The exposition of the second body of evidence will include the first at least two to four paragraphs explaining the overall nature of the second body of evidence. This is usually followed by three or four points describing, explaining, or providing more detail to give deeper meaning to the second body of evidence. In these pages as well, the student should include his own analysis statement(s) either within each of the subtopics or at the end of the exposition of the second body of evidence, whichever is appropriate for the evidence being presented.

Pages 8–9: The exposition of the third body of evidence should include at least two to four paragraphs explaining the overall nature of the third body of evidence. Three or more points describing, explaining, or providing more detail to give deeper meaning to the third body of evidence should also be included. A statement or statements of the student's own analysis should be provided within each of the subtopics or at the end of the exposition of the third body of evidence as well.

Page 10: In the conclusion, the student should tie together the evidence provided by his research. The conclusion should contain two paragraphs and not introduce any new information but connect the three bodies of evidence to each other and the thesis that the bodies of evidence have supported. The student may, however, suggest the path for future research.

Pages 11–12: Works Cited page(s) must include all borrowed material cited in the paper and be formatted correctly according to MLA style.

*The bodies of evidence are most often presented in descending order of importance, chronologically, or thematically. It is up to the student.*

### A Word on the Student's Analysis Statements

The student is using his researched information to support the thesis but the information is also helping to provide deeper meaning to his research subject. That deeper meaning allows his own thoughts and ideas to percolate from the borrowed materials. His new ideas allow him to connect with the culture and think critically about the research topic, just like some of the cultural critics he is reading.

The teacher and librarian are now aware of the student's material. At this point, prior to the student actually writing the paper, the teacher could ask for some examples of bodies of evidence from individual students, and model with that evidence some analysis statements that could be incorporated into the paper. Some workshop time should be allotted for modeling analysis statements. If possible during the workshop, each student should have written at least one analytical statement. Students should be made aware that the analysis statements indicate to the teacher what the student is thinking about the material he has borrowed and how it interacts with his thesis.

Suggested order of writing the paper:

## 1. Bodies of Evidence

The body of the paper in which the thesis is supported, should be written before the introduction. Students should take the notes that have been coded and categorized (in physical piles or in an organized written fashion of their choice) and prepare the three bodies of evidence. Writing this section before the introduction allows the student to develop the body of his paper by taking his notes and directly transforming them into cohesive arguments without a fixed, predetermined opening statement.

## 2. Conclusion

The conclusion should connect the three bodies of evidence to each other, if possible, and to the thesis statement that the bodies of evidence support. The conclusion should have no new information and should be brief. Two paragraphs are fine. If the student wishes or the teacher requests, a brief statement can be added about the path of future research in this topic.

## 3. Introduction

The introduction, which includes a definitive thesis statement determined by the student answering the articulated research question, should be written after the bodies of evidence have been presented. Before incorporating the thesis into the introduction the student should locate in his notes or his materials a startling, surprising, erudite, or provocative statement or quotation to serve as a "hook." That "hook" should grab the attention of the reader and serve as the opening salvo to the scholar's impressive discussion of the thesis.

**Handout #1: Writing the Paper** reflects virtually all of the materials in this overview.

## Workshop 17: Writing the Paper

**Learning Goals:** The goal of this workshop is to demystify the process of writing the humani-
ties research paper.
**Location:** Library or classroom
**Team:** Teacher, librarian, and writing resource guide
**Inquiry Unit:** The student is now preparing his paper in the Presentation Stage by using a sim-
ple suggested formula for structuring the presentation of evidence and preparing analytical
statements of that evidence.
**Total Time:** 50 minutes

| **Starter**<br>Time: 20 minute<br><br>Inquiry<br>Community | The teacher and librarian ask for a willing volunteer. If no vol-unteers are willing, a draft will be called to find two or three researchers who will serve as models. Each model's writing sample will follow the same process. The student will write on the board his outline and choose one of the three bodies of evi-dence to model.<br><br>With his outline and his notes he will begin to write sentences about the body of evidence he has chosen. He will aim to write one paragraph using borrowed information. Each of the three volunteers will do the same at the same time. After the para-graph is written, the first student will be asked to make an ana-lytical statement about the borrowed information and weave it into the paragraph.<br><br>The second student will be asked to complete his paragraph with an analytical statement. The third student will do the same after the second student is done.<br><br>Throughout this process the teacher, librarian, writing guide, or fellow students can help. **Handout #1: Writing the Paper** |
|---|---|
| **Work Time**<br>Time: 20 minute<br><br>Study Buddies | The group breaks up into study buddy pairs and each study buddy does the same activity and trades off, helping one another, critiquing one another, and lending emotional sup-port. The three guides should circulate and intervene when necessary. |
| **Reflection**<br>Time: 10 minute<br><br>Inquiry<br>Community | Any questions about the writing process should be addressed. |
| **Notes:** | Because this is one of the most difficult workshops, one or two unstructured work times may be called for. Individual assistance and tutorials may also be necessary. |

| Common Core Standards: | CCSS.ELA-LITERACY.W.9-10.7<br>Conduct short as well as more sustained research projects to answer a question (including a self-generated question) or solve a problem; narrow or broaden the inquiry when appropriate; synthesize multiple sources on the subject, demonstrating understanding of the subject under investigation.<br><br>CCSS.ELA-LITERACY.WHST.9-10.1.B<br>Develop claim(s) and counterclaims fairly, supplying data and evidence for each while pointing out the strengths and limitations of both claim(s) and counterclaims in a discipline-appropriate form and in a manner that anticipates the audience's knowledge level and concerns.<br><br>CCSS.ELA-LITERACY.W.9-10.1<br>Write arguments to support claims in an analysis of substantive topics or texts, using valid reasoning and relevant and sufficient evidence. |
|---|---|

# Workshop 17

## *Student Handout #1: Writing the Paper*

A formulaic approach for a ten page paper in the humanities:

Page 1: The heading, the title, the page number, and the introduction incorporating the hook and the thesis (2–4 paragraphs). If there is still room on page 1 begin the exposition of the first body of evidence. If not, begin on page 2.

Pages 2–4: In the exposition of the first body of evidence, the first at least two to four paragraphs will explain the overall nature of the first body of evidence and will usually be followed by three or four points describing, explaining, or providing more detail about the first body of evidence. In other words, these three points provide background and context that should be given in the body of evidence. Within each of the three bodies of evidence of the paper, the student should include some analysis statement(s) based upon his own growing knowledge and understanding of the subject. This can be done after the borrowed information has been stated.

Pages 5–7: The exposition of the second body of evidence will include the first at least two to four paragraphs explaining the overall nature of the second body of evidence. This is usually followed by three or four points describing, explaining, or providing more detail to give deeper meaning to the second body of evidence. In these pages as well, the student should include his own analysis statement(s) either within each of the subtopics or at the end of the exposition of the second body of evidence, whichever is appropriate for the evidence being presented.

Pages 8–9: The exposition of the third body of evidence should include at least two to four paragraphs explaining the overall nature of the third body of evidence. Three or more points describing, explaining, or providing more detail to give deeper meaning to the third body of evidence should also be included. A statement or statements of the student's own analysis should be provided within each of the subtopics or at the end of the exposition of the third body of evidence as well.

Page 10: In the conclusion, the student should tie together the evidence provided by his research. The conclusion should contain two paragraphs and not introduce any new information but connect the three bodies of evidence to each other and the thesis that the bodies of evidence have supported. The student may, however, suggest the path for future research.

Pages 11–12: Works Cited page(s) must include all borrowed material cited in the paper and be formatted correctly according to MLA style.

*The bodies of evidence are most often presented in descending order of importance, chronologically, or thematically. It is up to the student.*

Suggested order of writing the paper:

### 1. **Bodies of Evidence**

The body of the paper in which the thesis is supported should be written before the introduction. Take the notes that have been coded and categorized (in physical piles or in an organized written fashion of their choice) and prepare the three bodies of evidence. Writing this section before the introduction allows you to develop the body of your paper by taking your notes and directly transforming them into cohesive arguments without a fixed, predetermined opening statement.

### 2. **Conclusion**

The conclusion should connect the three bodies of evidence to each other, if possible, and to the thesis statement that the bodies of evidence support. The conclusion should have no new information and should be brief. Two paragraphs are sufficient. If you wish or your teacher requests, a brief statement can be added about the path of future research in this topic.

### 3. **Introduction**

The introduction, which includes a definitive thesis statement that was determined by the student answering the articulated research question, should be written after the bodies of evidence. Before incorporating the thesis into the introduction, you should locate in your notes or your materials a startling, surprising, erudite, or provocative statement or quotation to serve as a "hook." That "hook" should grab the attention of the reader and serve as the opening salvo to your impressive discussion of the thesis.

## Workshop 18

### Overview: Writing a Conclusion and Creating a "Cover Page"

The goal of the workshop is the student's understanding of the nature of a conclusion in a humanities research paper. A secondary goal is to learn the layout of the "cover page," which is the first page of the paper.

The teacher who is assigning the research paper may have some distinct expectations of what a conclusion should contain, but generally, the consensus is that it should contain no new information that has already not been incorporated into the body of the work. The paper should be brief and refer to the connections between the paper's thesis and the three bodies of evidence that "prove" or support and explain the thesis.

The role of the teacher in this workshop is truly one of a guide. Students are weary and the journey has been long. Writing a conclusion is an abstract practice and one that is not easy to explain. Sometimes the best way to approach a lesson such as this is simply to dive in.

As the teacher opens the workshop by silently writing on the board, "What did I learn from my research?" he is asking the student to explain to a complete stranger exactly what it is that was meaningful in the new information that the student encountered while conducting his research. Presumably, the main feature of what he learned became his thesis and the information he found formed his three bodies of evidence to support the thesis.

In the conclusion, the teacher is guiding the student to make *some* connections between these three already revealed bodies of evidence. These connections tie together the paper's narrative and thesis, lending deeper significance to the research.

Let us begin the workshop!

# Workshop 18: Writing a Conclusion and Creating a "Cover Page"

**Learning Goals:** The goal of this workshop is the student's understanding of the nature of a conclusion and the completion of the documents needed for a finished humanities research paper.

**Location:** Classroom

**Team:** Teacher and writing resource aide

**Inquiry Unit:** This workshop is part of the Presentation Stage of the ISP in which the student learns the elements necessary for a conclusion of a humanities research paper and how to compose a "cover page."

**Total Time:** 50 minutes

| | |
|---|---|
| **Starter**<br>Time: 10 minutes<br><br>Inquiry Community | The teacher comes to the front of the class and silently writes on the board, "What did you learn about your research subject from doing your research?" He tells the class that should a complete stranger ask, the student would have to reply. That reply becomes the first part of the conclusion and should reflect the thesis statement. One other thing the stranger might ask is, "How was your evidence connected to each other and your thesis?" The teacher distributes **Handout #1: Six Tips for Writing Your Conclusion** and asks a student volunteer to read the handout. The teacher will distribute a sample copy of a first page of a research paper in MLA style. What we call the "cover page" is the first page of the narrative of the humanities research paper and includes a heading with the name of student, name of teacher, name of course, and turn-in date on the left hand side. The title of the paper appears underneath the heading. |
| **Work Time**<br>Time: 30 minutes<br><br>Individual Scholars | Students following the tips in **Handout #1: Six Tips for Writing Your Conclusion**, and using the response they have given the teacher about the stranger's question, should prepare a draft conclusion that is two paragraphs long. Upon completion of the conclusion students should complete the "cover page." The title of the paper should incorporate some of the wording of the thesis. |
| **Reflection**<br>Time: 10 minutes<br><br>Inquiry Community | With the draft of the paper now essentially complete, the class should discuss how they feel about the work they have done and what lessons they have learned while doing it. The discussion should focus not on the content of the research but on the process. |
| **Notes:** | Students should be informed of the date of the next workshop, because at that workshop each student will present his study buddy with a copy of the draft of his research with all parts of the paper included. That workshop will consist of each study buddy peer-editing a research paper draft. |

| Common Core Standards: | CCSS.ELA-LITERACY.W.9-10.9<br>Draw evidence from literary or informational texts to support analysis, reflection, and research.<br><br>CCSS.ELA-LITERACY.WHST.9-10.2.F<br>Provide a concluding statement or section that follows from and supports the information or explanation presented (e.g., articulating implications or the significance of the topic).<br><br>CCSS.ELA-LITERACY.W.9-10.1.C<br>Use words, phrases, and clauses to link the major sections of the text, create cohesion, and clarify the relationships between claim(s) and reasons, between reasons and evidence, and between claim(s) and counterclaims. |
|---|---|

# Workshop 18

## *Student Handout #1: Six Tips for Writing Your Conclusion*

1. Do not repeat what you said in the body of your paper.

2. Do not introduce or refer to any new information that is not in your paper (even if it is in your notes).

3. Try to tie together the three bodies of evidence (your "proofs") and indicate how they are interconnected with your research thesis or how they support and give greater meaning to your research thesis.

4. Make your conclusion brief: two paragraphs.

5. Answer the question: "What did I learn in my research and how did my three bodies of evidence help to show this?"

6. The conclusion should be the narrative you compose about your research just prior to writing your introduction. The only tasks left are putting your "cover page" in order with your introduction and checking the paper to be sure your bibliography or works cited page(s) are complete.

## Workshop 19

## Overview: Preparing to Peer Edit the Draft

The goal of this lesson is to introduce students to the peer review process and to initiate a peer edit. At this point the student has found all his sources, made his notes, organized his notes, and fashioned an outline of his paper. Using his notes and his outline, he has put together his information to "answer" the research question that he has been developing and further specifying throughout his Information Search Process. With his research question fully formulated and answered into a thesis statement, he can now use the borrowed information to support his thesis by providing bodies of evidence for it, using multiple sources for each of the three bodies of evidence. In doing so he must fashion several paragraphs of narrative using his borrowed information to explain, give examples of, and/or show support for the thesis. Once done, he writes concluding remarks that tie together the three examples or evidence he has borrowed from his different sources. At this point he might also suggest the direction of future research. After finishing the conclusion he writes an introductory section for his paper that features a hook to grab the reader's attention and the thesis he has decided upon. The student then checks his document and his works cited page for the placement and accuracy of all citations for each note of borrowed material he used.

When the paper is put together and the research file, folder, or portfolio is ready, peer review of the draft can take place. Peer reviewers are other students who also are preparing their research papers. As such, they may not be experienced in peer editing and critique. The content teacher's responsibility is to provide clear-cut but brief instruction and standards for peer review, recognizing that in any class such review will have mixed results. However, most students take the responsibility to their peers quite seriously.

As this assignment is longer than most, we suggest a one-to-one study buddy peer review in which two students swap papers (in a quiet atmosphere) and read through the buddy's paper looking for the following:

### Content

1. Does the title make sense and give you a clue about the research paper?

2. Does the introduction familiarize the unknown reader by providing a history, a context, or some other idea that lends itself to making sense of the thesis?

3. Can you find the thesis and do you understand it?

4. Are there three or more developed ideas or examples to support the paper's thesis?

5. In the light of the above examples, does the conclusion of the paper tie the ideas together and are there any suggestions for further research?

## Style

1. Is the paper a whole paper with all of the parts?

2. Are the citations there?

3. Are the citations in the correct places?

4. Does every citation have a corresponding bibliographic entry on the works cited page(s)?

5. Is the cover page in good shape with all of the information on it?

6. Does each page have a "header," which is the last name of the paper's author and the page number of that particular page of the paper?

## Spelling and Grammar

1. Was the paper "spell checked"?

2. Can you find spelling errors?

3. Can you find grammatical errors of word use or punctuation?

4. Are the sentences complete sentences? That is, does each sentence have a subject and a verb?

5. Do the paragraphs make sense?

The key to peer review is twofold. First, the student critiquing is viewing the document (the research paper) through the eyes of his teenage peer and his critique has, therefore, the added weight of a peer. Second, the peer reviewer also learns about his own paper and its weaknesses while critiquing his peer's efforts. Enough time should be permitted for students to accomplish a thoughtful and careful peer review. **Handout #1: Critiquing Your Peer's Paper** will provide guidance. Comments by the peer about the paper can be written or given orally depending upon the preference of the teacher.

## Workshop 19: Preparing to Peer Edit the Draft

**Learning Goals:** The goal of this workshop is to introduce the student to the peer review process and initiate the peer review.

**Location:** Classroom

**Team:** Teacher, librarian, and resource guide for writing

**Inquiry Unit:** While this workshop is part of preparations for the presentation of the research paper, it also assumes the first role in assessing the paper through peer review.

**Total Time:** 50 minutes

| | |
|---|---|
| **Starter**<br>Time: 10 minutes<br><br>Inquiry Community | The teacher defines the peer review process and asks the students if they have ever peer reviewed a research paper. The teacher will distribute and review **Handout #1: Critiquing Your Peer's Paper** and remind students of the nature of constructive criticism as opposed to simply criticizing. |
| **Work Time**<br>Time: 30 minutes<br><br>Study Buddies | The students will sit with their study buddies and, using the handout, read, note, and critique the draft of the study buddy's paper. The critique can be done orally with each student pointing out both strong and weak points of the paper. The peer reviewer can also make specific notes on the paper. |
| **Reflection**<br>Time: 10 minute<br><br>Inquiry Community | The class gathers to reflect on the positive and negative aspects of the peer review process. A student volunteer can make notes on the board about the class discussion. |
| **Notes:** | Learning to critique a student paper, then actually critiquing the paper is a big undertaking. Another unstructured workshop would give the students more time to critique and share ideas.<br><br>The teacher and resource guide should continuously circulate to assist study buddy teams and be sure they stay on task. |
| **Common Core Standards:** | CCSS.ELA-LITERACY.W.9-10.5<br>Develop and strengthen writing as needed by planning, revising, editing, rewriting, or trying a new approach, focusing on addressing what is most significant for a specific purpose and audience. (Editing for conventions should demonstrate command of Language standards 1–3 up to and including grades 9–10.)<br><br>CCSS.ELA-LITERACY.SL.9-10.1.C<br>Propel conversations by posing and responding to questions that relate the current discussion to broader themes or larger ideas; actively incorporate others into the discussion; and clarify, verify, or challenge ideas and conclusions. |

# Workshop 19

## *Student Handout #1: Critiquing Your Peer's Paper*

As you begin to peer edit your peer's paper, look for the following items and try to answer all questions. You may make a list of notes or write directly on the paper.

### Content

1. Does the title make sense and give you a clue about the research paper?
2. Does the introduction familiarize the unknown reader by providing a history, a context, or some other idea that lends itself to making sense of the thesis?
3. Can you find the thesis and do you understand it?
4. Are there three or more developed ideas or examples to support the paper's thesis?
5. In the light of the above examples, does the conclusion of the paper tie the ideas together and are there any suggestions for further research?

### Style

1. Is the paper a whole paper with all of the parts?
2. Are the citations there?
3. Are the citations in the correct places?
4. Does every citation have a corresponding bibliographic entry on the works cited page(s)?
5. Is the cover page in good shape with all of the information on it?
6. Does each page have a "header" consisting of the last name of the paper's author and the page number of that particular page of the paper?

### Spelling and Grammar

1. Was the paper "spell checked"?
2. Can you find spelling errors?
3. Can you find grammatical errors of word use or punctuation?
4. Are the sentences full sentences? That is, does each sentence have a subject and a verb?
5. Do the paragraphs make sense?

# Research in the Assessment Stage of the Information Search Process

Workshop 20: Protocols for Turning in the Research Paper and Learning Portfolio

Only one workshop is planned for the Assessment Stage, to provide final instruction for turning in the research paper to the humanities teacher. At this stage the work of the student is complete and the hard work of the teacher and librarian begins as each student portfolio of paper notes or digital and backup documentation is reviewed and assessed one last time.

During this stage of the ISP, additional work time can be set aside for reflection by the students, which includes discussion about what was learned about the research subject and what was learned about the research process. Ideally, if time permits, an informal presentation can also be given by each student.

# Workshop 20

## Overview: Protocols for Turning in the Research Paper and Learning Portfolio

The goal of this less-structured workshop is the successful hand-over of the student's research paper and any or all materials that support the student's work. While protocols may vary from teacher to teacher or course to course, we are suggesting a portfolio approach in this workshop. A workshop plan is included although the workshop is primarily unstructured time.

Prior to evaluating a specifically structured and rather large research assignment, the teacher and librarian will use the student's portfolio for the research project to get a broad look at all sources used and all notes taken. The student's adherence to the instructions of each workshop can be viewed within the portfolio by reviewing all of the assignment handouts filled in or work annotated.

Students will use this unstructured workshop time to organize all materials, identify missing items, place materials in the order the handout suggests or in another order specified by the teacher, and make an extra copy of the research report in a paper/print iteration or in a separate digital file. The extra copy will then be accessible to the student should he need it. Missing items should be noted in the portfolio and replaced if the teacher requires. Each portfolio should contain, if possible, all print sources of shorter pieces or at least the title page of print sources for longer pieces, as well as copies of any pages of short digital pieces that were cited within the paper. Again, such research sources allow the evaluating teacher to better assess the student's work within the context of the source material used in the paper. The student's proper and full citations can be checked in the portfolio as well as within the paper itself. If a first draft is required and then corrected, the corrected draft used for the final paper should also be contained within the portfolio. The student **Handout #1: Checklist for Your Portfolio** will have a checklist of materials that should be placed within the portfolio. The portfolio itself should be properly labeled on the outside with a visible paper title, student name, course name, and teacher name.

**The number of copies of the paper that are included in the portfolio should be set by the teacher, depending upon how many people will evaluate the paper. One extra print copy of the paper should be retained by each student in case the portfolio is lost.**

# Workshop 20: Protocols for Turning in the Research Paper and Learning Portfolio

**Learning Goals:** The goal of this workshop is the organization and successful hand-over to the teacher of the research paper and portfolio.

**Location:** Classroom or library

**Team:** Teacher and librarian

**Inquiry Unit:** In this final unit, the student prepares his research for assessment prior to handing in the paper.

**Total Time:** 50 minutes

| | |
|---|---|
| **Starter**<br>Time: 10 minutes<br><br>Inquiry<br>Community | The teacher presents the students with homemade chocolate chip cookies and declares, "Today we will prepare our papers and portfolios to turn in to the teacher."<br><br>The teacher provides and reviews **Handout #1: Checklist for Your Portfolio.**<br><br>The teacher asks the students to gather all materials and give each other space to organize their individual portfolios. |
| **Work Time**<br>Time: 25 minutes<br><br>Individual<br>Scholars | Each student will begin to put together the materials on the checklist into the portfolio. The order of the materials will be written on the board and will follow the teacher's preference.<br><br>**Each portfolio should contain one extra printed copy of the entire paper to be retained by the student when the portfolio is turned in.** |
| **Reflection**<br>Time: 15 minutes<br><br>Study Buddies | Study buddy pairs will check each other's portfolios and note any missing pieces of the portfolio on a 3 x 5 notecard. |
| **Notes:** | This workshop demands a great deal of tabletop space for organizing the materials and creating the portfolio. Another unstructured workshop may be needed to complete the work. |

| Common Core Standards: | CCSS.ELA-LITERACY.WHST.9-10.1<br>Write arguments focused on *discipline-specific content.*<br><br>CCSS.ELA-LITERACY.WHST.9-10.1.D<br>Establish and maintain a formal style and objective tone while attending to the norms and conventions of the discipline in which they are writing.<br><br>CCSS.ELA-LITERACY.WHST.9-10.2.A<br>Introduce a topic and organize ideas, concepts, and information to make important connections and distinctions; include formatting (e.g., headings), graphics (e.g., figures, tables), and multimedia when useful to aiding comprehension.<br><br>CCSS.ELA-LITERACY.WHST.9-10.6<br>Use technology, including the Internet, to produce, publish, and update individual or shared writing products, taking advantage of technology's capacity to link to other information and to display information flexibly and dynamically. |

# Workshop 20

## *Student Handout #1: Checklist for Your Portfolio*

Depending upon the requirements of your humanities teacher, your portfolio could be a three ring binder, a notebook with inside pockets, a sturdy folder with ample inside pockets or even a digital folder. The checklist below includes all research materials required by your teacher and librarian to evaluate your research and its resulting paper. The order your teacher has you place the materials inside the portfolio is dependent upon the teacher's choice and will be on the board.

This is what must be in your portfolio, including all sources of materials you have used:

\_\_\_ All print sources of shorter pieces, annotated
\_\_\_ Title pages of print sources of longer pieces
\_\_\_ Copies of pages of short digital works, annotated
\_\_\_ Interrogation sheets with notes
\_\_\_ All handouts used in the research process
\_\_\_ All notes made
\_\_\_ Outline created
\_\_\_ First draft of paper with corrections (peer and/or teacher)
\_\_\_ Second or final draft of paper to include
    \_\_\_ First page ("cover page" with introductory narrative)
    \_\_\_ Body of paper with three major bodies of evidence
    \_\_\_ Conclusion of paper
    \_\_\_ Works cited page(s)
\_\_\_ Extra printed copy of final draft to be retained by the student.

# Appendices

# Appendix A

## Plan for Professional Development Workshop Session on the Guided Inquiry Approach to Teaching the Humanities Research Project

**Overview:** The following Professional Development (P.D.) is a three-hour session, intended for humanities teachers and information specialists who will work with students on the Humanities Inquiry Research Project. The ideal number of participants for this P.D. is 6–8 persons, total. The P.D. is rooted in Common Core-based curriculum and pedagogy has been piloted with staff of public and private high schools in New Jersey, New York, and Massachusetts. The pedagogy of this P.D. lesson reflects the student-centered style of the project itself.

---

**Objective:** Teachers and information specialists will be able to experience a model of the Humanities Inquiry Research Project; then anticipate challenges and design modifications for directing their own project in their school settings.

**Write Away:** *What does a "research" project typically consist of in your current humanities course? What would be different if the selection of topic, materials, and interrogation of sources was more centered on student interest and inquiry? What challenges can you foresee in allowing the project to be more student-centered? What benefits can you imagine for individual scholars?*

---

## Agenda

- Write Away – Individual (8 min.)
- Write Away Debrief and Discussion – Whole Group (7 min.)
- Selecting Our Own Humanities Topics and Reviewing with Peers (10 min.)
- Research Think/Pair/Share Protocol (30 min.)
- Developing (and Whole Group Share) of Guiding Question – Individual, Whole Group (15 min.)
- BREAK (10 min.)
- World Café Protocol on Some Lessons (30 min.)*
- World Café Protocol on Challenges and Benefits (Internal > External) – Small Groups (20 min.)*
- Individual Redesign (40 min.)
- Closing Circle (10 min.)

**Activities:** *Following a brief, silent write-away period, and whole group discussion, all participants will participate in the following activities (pair and small group activities should include a variety of teachers and information specialists in each group when possible).*

* EnageNY.org of the New York State Education Department.
Internet Expeditionary Learning Appendix: Protocols and Research.

**Selecting Our Own Humanities Topics and Reviewing With Peers:** *Teachers and information specialists mimic experience of students selecting and narrowing possible humanities topic of interest, under the guidance of P.D. facilitators. Technology to begin research should be made available. Participants should be reminded at this time, they need only identify and share topics of interest, and that after beginning research they will identify a guiding question, rather than a thesis.*

**Research Think/Pair/Share Protocol:** *Working in pairs, each participant should select and analyze the quality of two to three variant sources (ideally of different medium) for their topics. They discuss with partners those sources and their quality, as well as how to best interrogate each source. Partners should challenge one another to identify what questions and ideas can be drawn from each source selected.*

*Finding sources on shared databases (15 min.)*

- *Think/pair/share on quality and interrogation of sources (15 min.)*

**Developing (and Whole Group Share) of Guiding Questions:** *During this brief section of the P.D., each participant reflects on the previous activity, and narrows down their research topic to a guiding question. They are also asked to reflect on what challenges they foresee their own students having with this process, and strategies to address these potential pitfalls. In the last few minutes each teacher shares their topic, guiding question, and one potential pitfall an individual student may have with this process. During the break a list of these possible challenges is posted, and teachers are encouraged to provide one another feedback on sticky notes.*

- *Developing guiding questions (7 min.)*
- *Share out (8 min.)*
- *Break (10 min.)*

# World Café Protocols:

## Steps

1. Form three groups of three or four and sit together at a table.
2. Each group selects a "leader."
3. The leader's role is to record the major points of the conversation that takes place at the table and to then summarize the conversation using the recorded notes . . . a bit later.
4. The group discusses the topic at hand until time is called. Groups can be discussing the same topic or related topics.
5. The leader stays put; the rest of the group rotates to the next table.
6. The leader (the one who didn't move) presents a summary of the conversation recorded from the former group to the new group.
7. Each table selects a new leader.
8. Again, the new leader's role is to record the major points of the conversation that takes place at the table and to then summarize the conversation using the recorded notes . . . a bit later.
9. The group discusses the topic at hand until time is called.
10. Repeat the process, ideally until all participants have had a chance to lead.
11. After the final round, the last group of leaders present to the whole group rather than reporting out to a "next rotation."

*Source:* Gueswel, C. (2011, February 07). *Café Discussion Protocol.* Retrieved from http://elschools.org/commons/library/documents/1526

## Questions for First Cafe:

Round 1 – Look over some of the lessons: what questions come up?
Round 2 – What challenges do you foresee with some of the students?
Round 3 – How can you cater this lesson to make it more effective in your classroom?

## Questions for Second Café:

Round 1 – After looking at the unit, identify one student for whom this will be a challenge. What challenges do you see him/her having?
Round 2 – Focusing on the same student still, how can you help him/her identify an interest and hone that down to something more specific?
Round 3 – Focusing on the same student still, who are some partners in the school that could assist him/her?
Round 4 – Focusing on the same student, how can you help this student identify what would equate to a successful research question?

**Individual Redesign:** *Each participant—and certainly each school setting—should have identified, throughout the session, several challenges the project may present or necessary redesigns they would need to make, in order for these lessons to be highly successful in their own classrooms. This 40-minute session is a critical period for individuals to redesign lessons and material with appropriate modifications for their students and classroom/school setting. Facilitators should circulate, assisting individual participants, and pairing like challenges, in order to brainstorm strategies. Each participant should have redesigned at least one lesson for their own classroom by the end of this section of the P.D.*

**Closing Circle:** *This final section is designed as a space for all participants to reflect on the lessons, the professional development itself, and share what they have learned (both positive and critical) that will help them in implementing this project in their own classrooms. It should be an open conversation, and all participants should give input before finishing the P.D.*

# Appendix B

## How to Use the Instruments in the SLIM Packet

The School Library Impact Measure (SLIM) packet was developed by Rutgers University scholars to measure the effects of trained librarians and the Guided Inquiry approach to student learning. A questionnaire (the SLIM instrument) was devised to gather data on student learning and affective behaviors displayed by students at three points in the information search process. Initially the instrument is given when the student selects a topic but before completing much research. The second instrument (whose language is like the first instrument) is administered midway through the research—just around the formulation stage. The third instrument (whose language is more in the past tense) is administered at the end of the information search process after the paper has been turned in to the teacher but before the paper has been assessed. The instruments are completed while the information is fresh in the student's head. At each administration of the instrument, the students use no notes or materials. They may ask questions of the teacher but they must individually fill out the instrument. The exercise usually takes twenty to thirty minutes of a class period. Students should be told this is *not* a test and will not be graded like a test, although a teacher may choose to give points for effort, honesty, and full participation to indicate that effort.

# The School Library Impact Measure (SLIM) Packet

## Instrument #1

Class _____   Teacher _____

Name _____   Date _____

**Write the title that best describes your research topic at this time:**

_____

_____

_____

_____

_____

_____

**Your task:**

Take some time to think about your chosen topic. Now write down what you know about this topic. When you write down your ideas, use as many words, phrases, and sentences that come to mind that show what you know about your topic.

_____

_____

_____

_____

_____

_____

_____

_____

_____

**Why have you chosen this topic?** _____

_____

_____

_____

_____

_____

From Todd, R., Kuhlthau, C., & Heinstrom, J. (2005). *School library impact measure reflection instruments and scoring guidelines*. Center for International Scholarship in School Libraries at Rutgers University. Reprinted with permission.

**Describe how much you think you know about this topic:**   Expert Knowledge ( )
Know a Lot ( )    Know Some Stuff ( )    Know a Little ( )    Know Nothing at All ( )


**Write down what you think you will enjoy the <u>most</u> about researching your topic:**

_____

_____

_____

_____

_____


**Write down what you think you will enjoy the <u>least</u> about researching your topic:**

_____

_____

_____

_____

_____


**How are you feeling about your project? Why?** _____

_____

_____

_____

_____

_____

From Todd, R., Kuhlthau, C., & Heinstrom, J. (2005). *School library impact measure reflection instruments and scoring guide-lines.* Center for International Scholarship in School Libraries at Rutgers University. Reprinted with permission.

## Instrument #2

Class _____   Teacher _____

Name _____   Date _____

**Write the title that best describes your research topic at this time, midpoint in your research:** _____

_____

_____

_____

_____

_____

**Your task:**

Take some time to think about your chosen topic. Now write down what you now know about this topic. When you write down your ideas, use as many words, phrases, and sentences that come to mind that show what you know about your topic. (**You may add material on the back of this sheet.**)

_____

_____

_____

_____

_____

_____

_____

_____

_____

_____

**Why have you chosen this topic?** _____

_____

_____

_____

_____

From Todd, R., Kuhlthau, C., & Heinstrom, J. (2005). *School library impact measure reflection instruments and scoring guidelines.* Center for International Scholarship in School Libraries at Rutgers University. Reprinted with permission.

**Describe how much you think you know about this topic:**   Expert Knowledge ( )
Know a Lot ( )   Know Some Stuff ( )   Know a Little ( )   Know Nothing at All ( )


**Write down what you think you are enjoying the <u>most</u> about researching your topic:**

_____

_____

_____

_____

_____

_____


**Write down what you are enjoying the <u>least</u> about researching your topic:**

_____

_____

_____

_____

_____

_____


**How are you feeling about your project? Why?**   _____

_____

_____

_____

_____

_____

_____

## Instrument #3

Class _____   Teacher _____

Name _____   Date _____

**Write the title that best described your research topic at the time of your presentation:**

_____

_____

_____

_____

_____

**Your task:**

Take some time to think about your chosen topic. Now write down what you now know about this topic. When you write down your ideas, use as many words, phrases, and sentences that come to mind that show what you know about your topic.

_____

_____

_____

_____

_____

_____

_____

_____

_____

_____

**Why did you choose this topic?** _____

_____

_____

_____

_____

From Todd, R., Kuhlthau, C., & Heinstrom, J. (2005). *School library impact measure reflection instruments and scoring guidelines.* Center for International Scholarship in School Libraries at Rutgers University. Reprinted with permission.

**Describe how much you think you know about this topic:**   Expert Knowledge ( )
Know a Lot ( )    Know Some Stuff ( )    Know a Little ( )   Know Nothing at All ( )

**Write down what you enjoyed the <u>most</u> about researching your topic:**

_____

_____

_____

_____

_____

**Write down what you enjoyed the <u>least</u> about researching your topic:**

_____

_____

_____

_____

_____

**How are you feeling about your project? Why?** _____

_____

_____

_____

_____

_____

# Appendix C

## Interrogation of Source Sheet Rubric

Student's Name _____

Topic _____

Name of Interrogation sheet _____

| Points Given | Very Good 2 points | Acceptable 1 point | Not Acceptable ½ point |
|---|---|---|---|
| Identification of source | | | |
| Content of answers to questions (quantity) | | | |
| Depth/breadth of answers to questions (quality) | | | |
| Analysis/interpretation of content | | | |

Extra credit for exceptional interrogation job (up to 2 points)

Comments on interrogation _____

_____

_____

_____

_____

Total points for interrogation of source _____

# The Humanities Research Project

## Research Paper Final Draft Evaluation Sample A

Student's Name _____

## Content

Organization of Support (20 pts.) _____

_____

Development of Research Question/Thesis/Extent of Research (20 pts.) _____

_____

Use of Examples (10 pts.) _____

_____

## Mechanics

Works Cited Page (10 pts.) _____

_____

Paragraph Organization (10 pts.) _____

_____

In-text Parenthetical Citations (10 pts.) _____

_____

Use of Transitions (10 pts.) _____

_____

Spelling/Punctuation (5 pts.) _____

_____

Sentence Structure (5 pts.) _____

_____

**Subtotal for final draft:** _____

**Final Draft Grade (out of 100)** _____

Adapted by Andrew Lutz, Gill St. Bernard's
10th Grade American Studies Research Project, 2014

# The Humanities Research Project

## Overall Research Project Evaluation Sample B

Student's Name _____

Topic _____


## *Research Grade*

Five Sources with Notebook (5 pts.) _____

_____

Initial Notes (20 pts.) _____

_____

Research Question (5 pts.) _____

_____

Last Sources (5 pts. ) _____

_____

Final Notes (20 pts.) _____

_____

Thesis (5 pts.) _____

_____

Outline (20 pts.) _____

_____

Rough Draft (20 pts.) _____


## *Paper Grade*

Final Draft of the Paper Grade (100 pts.) _____

_____


**Total (out of 200 pts.)** _____

Adapted by Andrew Lutz, Gill St. Bernard's
10th Grade American Studies Research Project, 2014

# Works Cited

Arendt, Hannah. *The Human Condition*. 2nd ed. Chicago: U of Chicago, 1998. Print.

Armstrong, Kristen. *Interrogating a Sporting Event*. 17 Dec. 2014. Print. Gill St. Bernard's School, Gladstone, NJ.

Belkin, Nicholas J. "Anomalous States of Knowledge as a Basis for Information Retrieval." *Canadian Journal of Information Science* (1980): 133–43. Print.

Bolter, Jay David, and Richard Grusin. *Remediation: Understanding New Media*. Cambridge, MA: MIT, 2000. Print.

Bostian, Lawrence. *Interrogating a Natural Phenomenon*. 17 Dec. 2014. Print. Gill St. Bernard's School, Gladstone, NJ.

Brolund, Goran. *Interrogating a Legal Document*. 17 Dec. 2014. Print. Fyrisskolan, Uppsala, Sweden.

Buckingham, David. *Media Education: Literacy, Learning, and Contemporary Culture*. Cambridge, UK: Polity, 2003. Print.

Canada, Paul. *Interrogating a Garment*. 17 Dec. 2014. Print. Gill St. Bernard's School, Gladstone, NJ.

*The Center for Media Justice: Media Rights, Access, & Representation—For Everyone*. The Center for Media Justice, n.d. Web. 15 Dec. 2014.

Conley, David T. "Rethinking the Notion of 'Noncognitive.'" *Education Week*, 22 Jan. 2013. Web.

Demontigny, Isabelle. Personal interview. Interview by Emilia Giordano. 17 Dec. 2014.

Diamond, Jennifer. *Interrogating a Coin or Pottery Sherd*. 17 Dec. 2014. Print. Gill St. Bernard's School, Gladstone, NJ.

Diamond, William. *Interrogating a Live or Recorded Speech or Transcript of a Speech*. 17 Dec. 2014. Print. Gill St. Bernard's School, Gladstone, NJ.

Dubrow Branch, Abbe. Personal interview. Interview by Randell Schmidt. 6 Nov. 2014.

Easybib. *MLA Examples of Popular Sources*. New York: Easybib, n.d. PDF.

Fitzgerald, Lee. *Interrogating a Textual Source of Nonfiction*. 17 Dec. 2014. Print. Charles Sturt University, Wagga Wagga, Australia.

Gardner, Howard. *The Disciplined Mind: What All Students Should Understand*. New York: Simon & Schuster, 1999. Print.

Gardner, Howard. *Frames of Mind: The Theory of Multiple Intelligences*. New York: Basic, 2011. Print.

Giordano, Emilia N. *Interrogating Social Media Content*. 17 Dec. 2014. Print. Gill St. Bernard's School, Gladstone, NJ.

Gueswel, C. "Cafe Discussion Protocol." *Expeditionary Learning*. 07 Feb. 2011. Web. Apr. 2015.

Hesler, Claudia. *Databases for the Humanities Research Paper (Sample)*. 17 Dec. 2014 Gill St. Bernard's School, Gladstone, NJ.

Hesler, Claudia. *List of Resources for a Humanities Research Paper (Sample)*. 17 Dec. 2014 Gill St. Bernard's School, Gladstone, NJ.

"History Standards." *Welcome to UCLA's National Center for History in the Schools.* UCLA Department of History, National Center for History in Schools, n.d. Web. 21 Jan. 2015.

Isusi, Sarah. *Interrogating a Piece of Artwork.* 17 Dec. 2014. Print. Gill St. Bernard's School, Gladstone, NJ.

Jenkins, Henry. "Confronting the Challenges of Participatory Culture: Media Education for the 21st Century." *Jenkins White Paper PDF.* Massachusetts Institute of Technology/MacArthur Foundation, 2006. Web. 12 May 2015.

Kuhlthau, Carol Collier. *Seeking Meaning: A Process Approach to Library and Information Services.* Westport, CT: Libraries Unlimited, 2004. Print.

Kuhlthau, Carol Collier, Ann K. Caspari, and Leslie K. Maniotes. *Guided Inquiry: Learning in the 21st Century.* Westport, CT: Libraries Unlimited, 2007. Print.

Law, John. "Notes on the Theory of the Actor-Network: Ordering, Strategy, and Heterogeneity." *Systems Practice* 5.4 (1992): 379–93. Web.

Lutz, Andrew, comp. *Research Paper Final Draft Evaluation.* 17 Dec. 2014. Print. Gill St. Bernard's School, Gladstone, NJ.

Lutz, Andrew. *Interrogating Realistic Fiction.* 17 Dec. 2014. Print. Gill St. Bernard's School, Gladstone, NJ.

Lutz, Andrew. *Overall Research Project Evaluation.* 17 Dec. 2014. Print. Gill St. Bernard's School, Gladstone, NJ.

Martin, Derek. *Interrogating an Allusion.* 17 Dec. 2014. Print. Gill St. Bernard's School, Gladstone, NJ.

Martinez, Michael E. "What Is Metacognition?" *Phi Delta Kappan* May 2006: 69–99. Web.

Modern Language Association. *MLA Handbook for Writers of Research Papers.* 7th ed. New York: Modern Language Association of America, 2009. Print.

Müller, Jörg. E-mail message to author. 21 Oct. 2014.

Orr, Cynthia. *Interrogating a Graph.* 17 Dec. 2014. Print. Gill St. Bernard's School, Gladstone, NJ.

Ort, Robert. *Interrogating a Photograph.* 17 Dec. 2014. Print. Gill St. Bernard's School, Gladstone, NJ.

Prensky, Marc. "Digital Natives, Digital Immigrants Part 1." *On the Horizon* 9.5 (2001): 1–6. Web. 10 Dec. 2014.

"Preparing America's Students for Success." *Common Core State Standards Initiative,* 2015. Web. 21 Jan. 2015.

Ripton, John. *Interrogating a Political Cartoon.* 2 May 2014. Print. Gill St. Bernard's School, Gladstone, NJ.

Schiesswohl, Margery. *Interrogating a Live or Recorded Theater Performance.* 17 Dec. 2014. Print. Gill St. Bernard's School, Gladstone, NJ.

Schmidt, Geoffrey M. *Professional Development Unit on a Guided Inquiry Project.* 17 Dec. 2014. Print. Phoenix Charter Academy, Springfield, MA.

Schmidt, Joseph H. *Historical Resources for the Humanities (Compliation).* Np. New York, NY, 2014. Print.

Schmidt, Randell K. *A Guided Inquiry Approach to High School Research.* Santa Barbara, CA: Libraries Unlimited, 2013. Print.

Schmidt, Randell K., Maureen M. Smyth, and Virginia K. Kowalski. *Teaching the Scientific Literature Review: Collaborative Lessons for Guided Inquiry.* Second Edition. Santa Barbara, CA: Libraries Unlimited, 2014. Print.

Schmitt, Maribeth Cassidy, and Timothy J. Newby. "Metacognition: Relevance to Instructional Design." *Journal of Instructional Development* 9.4 (1986): 29–33. Web.

Shanahan, Timothy, and Cynthia Shanahan. "What Is Disciplinary Literacy and Why Does It Matter?" *Topics in Language Disorders* 32.1 (2012): 7–18. Web. 17 Dec. 2014.

Short, James E. *How Much Media? 2013 Report on American Consumers.* U of Southern California Marshall School of Business, 2013. Print.

Southerland, David. *Interrogating a Live or Recorded Musical Performance.* 17 Dec. 2014. Print. Gill St. Bernard's School, Gladstone, NJ.

Tierney, Amy M., and Randell K. Schmidt. *Interrogating in an Interview.* 17 Dec. 2014. Print. Gill St. Bernard's School, Gladstone, NJ.

Todd, Ross, Carol Kuhlthau, and Jannica Heinstrom. *Impact Studies - SLIM - CISSL.* Center for International Scholarship in School Libraries at Rutgers University, 2012. Web. 22 Jan. 2015.

Trainin, Guy, and Lee H. Swanson. "Cognition, Metacognition, and Achievement of College Students with Learning Disabilities." *Learning Disability Quarterly* 28.4 (2005): 261–72. Print.

Wineburg, Samuel S., Daisy Martin, and Chauncey Monte-Sano. *Reading Like a Historian: Teaching Literacy in Middle and High School History Classrooms.* New York: Teachers College, Columbia U, 2013. Print.

World Cafe Protocol. EngageNY.org of the New York State Department of Education, Expeditionary Learning Appendix and Protocols. Web. 29 Oct. 2014.

# Index

# About the Authors

**RANDELL K. SCHMIDT** is the head librarian at Gill St. Bernard's School in Gladstone, New Jersey. Her published work includes ABC-CLIO's *A Guided Inquiry Approach to High School Research*. She is also the lead author of *Teaching the Scientific Literature Review: Collaborative Lessons for Guided Inquiry*, second edition. She holds a bachelor's degree from Hanover College, a master of divinity degree from Princeton Theological Seminary, and a master of library service degree from Rutgers University.

**EMILIA N. GIORDANO** is an assistant librarian at Gill St. Bernard's School in Gladstone, New Jersey. She holds a bachelor's degree in Liberal Studies with a concentration in media and is a master's degree candidate in Media Studies with a focus on Participatory Learning and Digital Media from The New School for Public Engagement in New York City. Emilia has taught the scientific literature review at the high school level and a ninth-grade Guided Inquiry in basic research skills course. She has taught humanities research skills to tenth-grade students. On all high school levels, Emilia has integrated media literacy instruction to promote information and digital literacies, and to encourage media activism and civic engagement.

**GEOFFREY M. SCHMIDT** is current director of School Culture and former director of Curriculum and Instruction at Phoenix Charter Academy (PCA) in Springfield, Massachusetts. Before joining the PCA Springfield team as a founding administrator, Geoffrey was an ELA teacher and department leader in New York City's District 79, at Innovation Diploma Plus High School, and at ROADs Charter High School, in Brooklyn, New York. He is a proud member of the founding cohort of Lehigh University's Urban Principal's Academy (U*PAL). Geoffrey has a passion for providing equitable and social justice-oriented curriculum, instruction, and school culture to students previously disengaged from their own education.

# A Guided Inquiry Approach to Teaching the Humanities Research Project